PORTUS LONDINII

CM MCMLXXXV

THE PORT OF ROMAN LONDON

Gustav Milne

B.T. Batsford Ltd   London

Typeset by Servis Filmsetting Ltd, Manchester
and printed in Great Britain by
Anchor Brendon Ltd, Tiptree, Essex

for the publishers
Batsford Academic and Educational, an imprint of
B.T. Batsford Ltd
4 Fitzhardinge Street
London W1H 0AH

British Library Cataloguing in Publication Data
Milne, Gustav
   The Roman port of London.
   1. London (England)—Harbour—History
   2. Rome—History—Empire, 30 B.C.–476 A.D.
   I. Title
   387.1'09362'1   HE558.L8

ISBN 0 7134 4364 2 (cased)
ISBN 0 7134 4365 0 (limp)

CONTENTS

PREFACE

The earliest surviving mention of London comes from Cornelius Tacitus (AD 55–*c*120). Referring to the rebellion in AD 60, he described London as a settlement which did not rank as a 'colonia', 'but was an important centre for businessmen and merchandise' (*Londinium . . . cognomento quidem coloniae non insigne, sed copia negotiatorum et commeatuum maxime celebre*) (Grant, 1956, 319). This incidental comment has exercised a powerful influence on the later study of the Roman city, providing the basis for the almost universally accepted view that trade and commerce was the life blood of the town throughout the period of the Roman occupation. Unfortunately, Tacitus never visited Britain, although his source, Julius Agricola, had served in the Province in *c*AD 70, returning as governor in AD 78–84. Nevertheless, since Tacitus wrote his version of mid-first-century events in the second century, his comments should invite caution. Indeed, present-day archaeologists have actually seen more of Roman London than Tacitus ever did, and have recorded more phases of occupation than even Agricola saw.

Although London was once both the capital and the largest town in the Roman province of Britannia, a clear picture of its development in that crucial 400-year period is not found in the documentary record. This is because there are only ten surviving references to *Londinium* by classical writers, the total information amounting to a mere six printed pages including translations (*RCHM* 1928, 1–7). A detailed understanding of Roman London must therefore be based primarily on the archaeological evidence, the physical remains of the ancient city which lie, or rather lay, beneath London's basements and streets. This source material is hard evidence, the tangible, physical remains of the settlement, as eloquent and informative as any written chronicle, provided that it can be correctly interpreted. Unfortunately, such is the pace of growth in the City that most of these invaluable deposits have already been destroyed by the deep foundations required for modern redevelopment. It was, however, possible to examine and record a sample of the sites, including some on the waterfront, before the crucial information they contained was lost for ever.

This book is an assessment of recent excavations on the London waterfront near London Bridge and Billingsgate, investigations which produced graphic evidence for the development and decline of London's first major harbour complex. The full archive reports generated by those excavations are housed in the Museum of London library where they may be consulted on request. This summary of that rich body of data is therefore an account of evidence which forms the vital first chapter in the economic history of the City, and hopefully stands as one of the most detailed appraisals of a provincial Roman port yet undertaken. At a more general level, it is also a study of the pressures, principles and purpose of urban archaeology in the late twentieth century. As such, it attempts to demonstrate that these salvage rescue excavations can provide valuable research archives, the interpretation of which contributes positively to our history.

The book was conceived as a complement to recent general surveys of the Roman town (eg Marsden 1980; Morris 1982; Merrifield 1983), for the approach adopted is quite different. It concentrates on a specific aspect of Roman London, its harbour, in the hope that this detailed examination will throw fresh light not only on the status and role of the whole city, but also on the validity of the interpretations put upon Tacitus' celebrated description.

But first the data must be collected and collated, and to do this requires work, hard work, but above all, team work. It is not possible to name all those who have helped with the excavation of the Roman waterfront sites, with the compilation of the detailed archive reports or with the processing of the finds and samples, but Patrick Allen, Ian Blair, David Bowler, Mark Burch, Peter Cardiff, Prince Chitwood, Phillip Claris, Anne Davis, Barbara

Davies, Sarah Dilane, Val Horsman, Wendy Horton, Pete James, Michael Jones, Alison McQuitty, Patrick Newell, Brian Pye, Jez Reeve, Caroline Rochester, Sandra Rose, Alison Taylor, Kirsten Taylor and Hester White were just some of the professional staff who made notable contributions to the project. They were ably supported by many enthusiastic volunteers and the dedicated membership of Pip Thompson's City of London Archaeological Society. Access to the main sites considered in this book was negotiated by Brian Hobley and John Schofield, and the co-operation of many tolerant site agents and sub-contractors is gratefully acknowledged.

This project has benefitted from the work of several specialists, notably Dr Battarbee (University College, London), Jennifer Hillam (Sheffield University), Alison Locker (Ancient Monuments Laboratory), Vanessa Straker (Bristol University) and Jessica Winder (Southampton University).

The production of the book itself also incorporates the efforts of many members of the Museum of London, particularly Nick Bateman and Christine Milne, and the other contributors whose work is itemised on the contents page. They include Francis Grew, Jenny Hall, Louise Miller (who prepared all the data from the Miles Lane site for this publication), Frances Pritchard and Beth Richardson, while the section on Building 6 in Chapter 11 includes work by Chris Guy, and the coin report in Chapter 3 contains a note on conservation by Helen Ganniaris. All had previously worked directly or indirectly on the waterfront project. The photos of the Museum of London's Roman harbour model were taken by John Edwards and the rest of the photography was by Trevor Hurst, Jon Bailey and Jan Scrivener, with the exception of Figs. 52 and 70, published by permission of the British Museum; Fig. 64, by permission of the National Maritime Museum; and Fig. 67 by permission of the Historic Buildings and Monuments Commission. The rest of the illustrations were compiled and drawn by Christine Milne, apart from Fig. 46, drawn by Nick Griffiths who also helped with Fig. 71; Fig. 59 by R. Embleton; Figs. 65, 68 and 69 drawn by Anne Sutton; Fig. 66 by David Parfitt, and Fig. 68 by John Pearson. Other assistance was given by Alison Blake, Richard Lea and Paul Tyers.

Much helpful advice was given by Tony Dyson, and useful comments were also received from many other colleagues in the Museum of London, including Dr H. Chapman, Peter Marsden, Mike Rhodes, and John Schofield. Professor Frere (Oxford University), Dr Fulford (Reading University), Dr Limbrey (Birmingham University) and Professor Rickman (University of St Andrews) also kindly discussed various parts of the text. Nevertheless, mistakes and misinterpretations which remain are the responsibility of the authors.

Last but by no means least, acknowledgement must be made for the great interest in the work shown by the English Property Corporation, National Provident Institution, Land Securities (Management) Ltd, Verronworth and Vitiglade Ltd, and subsequently, the Department of the Environment (now the Historic Buildings and Monuments Commission), who generously provided the financial support without which the evidence would have been lost forever.

The royalties from the sale of this book go to the City of London Archaeological Trust Fund.

This book is dedicated to the memory of Caroline Rochester who worked on the London waterfront projects from 1981 to 1983.

DEATH OF A VICTORIAN PORT

It is a sad irony that some of the spoil used to infill London's derelict nineteenth-century docks in 1980 contained well-preserved timbers from an even older harbour complex. The ancient structures had been disturbed and destroyed during the extensive development of Thameside sites within the City itself. The following year saw archaeologists excavating and recording evidence of London's first landing stage, bridge and warehouses near Pudding Lane just as the closure of the Royal Docks was announced, marking the final demise of Dockland. These two events, the ignominious fate of London's enclosed docks and the rediscovery of its Roman harbour, are linked by more than the coincidence of date. Both were part of the transformation undergone by the Port of London in the late twentieth century, as a brief summary of the port's history shows.

The main Roman harbour was established in the first century AD on the north bank of the Thames near the present site of London Bridge. The port expanded dramatically up to the early third century, but seems to have contracted thereafter. Recent research suggests that the Saxon settlement which developed west of the City walls in the Aldwych area replaced Roman London as a major commercial centre by the eighth century (Vince 1984). However, the fear of Viking raids in the ninth century may have encouraged the population to reoccupy the more readily defensible walled site of Roman London. Subsequently, the city was redeveloped as a major port from the tenth century onwards, but in the early eighteenth century the length of the 'legal quays' upon which all cargoes had to be discharged and cleared by Customs only totalled c430m. This was insufficient to accommodate the contemporary vessels and cargoes from Europe, Africa, the Americas and the East, and by the early nineteenth century the system of enclosed docks was inaugurated to remedy the situation (Pudney 1975). By c1830 the Port of London had spread to Blackwall, by c1880 to Woolwich and by 1886 to Tilbury. However, the riverside wharves on both banks of the Thames within the old City continued to profit from the ever increasing trade coming to London, for they were serviced by lighters loaded from vessels berthed in the enclosed docks and then towed up river (Fig. 1).

After World War II, the badly blitzed docks were not rebuilt on the old Victorian lines but tried to adapt to the new innovations of the 1950s and 1960s, from forklift trucks to containerisation. But successful ports in the 1970s and 1980s had to provide deep-water berths suitable for supertankers and the facilities and space necessary to handle at speed containers and other bulk commodities, making use of the latest non-labour-intensive methods (Fig. 2). The majority of London's enclosed docks (many of which were built in the age of sailing ships) did not and could not meet these demanding criteria. They have now been closed. As a direct result the up-river wharves and warehouses in the City which once prospered on traffic from the docks were left derelict.

For a thousand years London had been the leading port in the land, and had once been the largest in the world. Today the unthinkable has happened: the City is no longer a port at all. Pleasure boats are now almost the only craft to be seen on otherwise deserted reaches of the river which once swarmed with tugs and lighters. The riverside wharves and warehouses have been demolished or converted for other purposes; the St Katharine's, London, Surrey and East India Docks were closed from 1968–71; and the Milwall, West India, Victoria, Albert and King George V Docks from 1980–1. The Port of London Authority now operates from Tilbury, some 25 miles east of the City, and the total tonnage handled by them in 1982 was less than that at Shetland in Scotland. The principal container and roll-on/roll-off ports in Britain in that year were Dover and Felixstowe, with 'London' (ie Tilbury) third (Dept. of Transport 1982, 74).

1 *Handling cargoes in the London Docks in the inter-war years: goods carried by these sea-going ships were laboriously transferred onto lighters which were then towed to the upriver warehouses on the City waterfront.*

2 *Handling cargoes today: metal weather-proof containers loaded directly onto lorries or trains, bypassing the need for the waterfront warehouses.*

3 *The City of London is no longer an internationally-famous port. Since 1960, extensive redevelopment saw acres of obsolete nineteenth-century waterfront warehousing demolished, exposing the remains of an even earlier harbour complex hidden beneath the basements.*

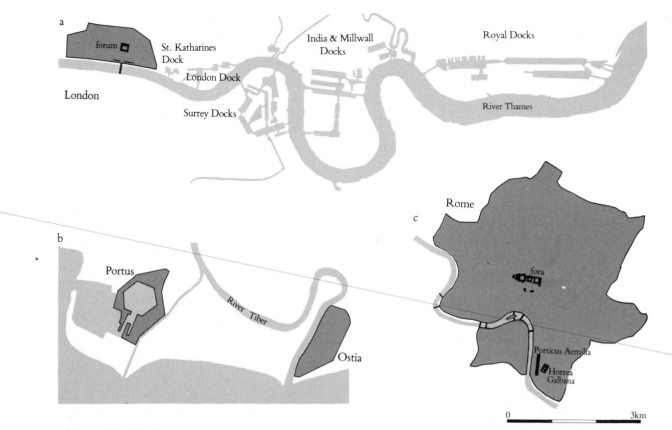

4 *London's Roman harbour in perspective. The maximum extent of the nineteenth-century enclosed docks reflected the size of the British Empire and London's leading position in it. The provincial Roman harbour within the City (south of the forum) is clearly dwarfed by its nineteenth-century successor and by the ancient harbour installations at Portus and Ostia, near Rome. Also note the size of warehousing in the Aventine, the harbour area on the River Tiber, in Rome itself.*

The discovery of a Roman harbour

In the wake of this startling transformation (Fig. 3), the obsolete warehousing on the City's waterfront which had escaped the Blitz was swept away and replaced by two massive telecommunications centres and a plethora of banks and office accommodation. However, in the early 1970s archaeologists from the Museum of London (formerly the Guildhall Museum) began conducting excavations on many of these waterfront sites in advance of their imminent destruction (Milne and Milne 1979). As a result, part of the ancient Roman harbour was discovered: an ambitious scheme which, like its nineteenth-century successor, expanded rapidly, flourished and failed (Fig. 4). It is this remarkable evidence of London's earliest major harbour complex which is described in this book.

No archaeological evidence for a substantial pre-Roman settlement has been recorded in the area now occupied by the City, and it is generally accepted that the town was founded in the mid-first century AD (Dyson and Schofield 1981, 25).

However, there has been considerable dispute as to whether this was the result of military or mercantile enterprise. An assessment of harbour development in Roman London is a necessary complement to the evidence already amassed from other sources on this issue, and indeed to many other basic interpretations of London's growth and role.

But before the story could be told, the harbour had to be found. That it had once existed and had played a vital role in the development of the provincial capital was universally agreed, but exactly where the main quays were, and, more practically, whether any trace of them survived, were crucial questions demanding answers. For example, one commentator argued that the mouth of the Walbrook, a stream which flows into the Thames at Dowgate may have been the centre of commercial activity (Merrifield 1965); another suggested that the larger ships would have berthed in Barking c19km to the east of the City (Morris 1982, 269–70).

Roman London was much smaller than the vast conurbation of about eight million people in the thirty-two boroughs that constitute London today, although it became the largest town in the province of Britannia. The City wall built in AD 200 enclosed an area on the north bank of the Thames stretching from what is now the Tower of London to Blackfriars, and from the Barbican to Aldgate. An extensive suburb developed on the opposite bank of the river in Southwark at the southern end of the Roman bridge. The precise position of that bridge (or bridges?) has been the subject of considerable debate. Its location is of considerable importance to an understanding of the City's history, not least because it would have marked the heart of the Roman harbour: the point above which large sea-going vessels could not have passed. The famous medieval bridge, built in 1176–1209 and much modified thereafter, ran from St Magnus church on the north bank to what is now Hay's Wharf on the south. When it was demolished and replaced by Rennie's bridge, the dredging involved in this redevelopment in 1824–31 brought up a remarkable concentration of Roman finds in the vicinity. It was therefore suggested that the Roman bridge must have occupied a very similar site to that of its medieval successor (Roach-Smith 1859, 21–2).

In the same period, chestnut and oak piles supporting hurdlework revetments were observed during the construction of the bridge abutment in 1831 (Merrifield 1965, 284). This was thought to represent part of a Roman waterfront structure, and a similar feature was noted at the foot of Botolph Lane in 1834 (Merrifield 1965, 286). A network of piles and transverse beams c450mm square extending across Thames Street was recorded in 1868 when the foundations for Cannon Street Station were being laid. Contemporary comment held that the timbers 'doubtless formed the old waterline and Thames embankment forming the southern part of Roman London' (Price 1870, 74–5). By 1885 sufficient evidence had been collected to suggest that the river level in the Roman period was considerably lower than at the present day. Further advances were made in the 1920s with the publication of Sir Mortimer Wheeler's essay on Roman London (RCHM 1928) and the discovery of extensive areas of substantial interlaced timberwork on sites either side of Miles Lane, close to London Bridge. These were associated with masonry buildings and with a large dump of burnt Samian pottery thought to represent the clearance of a second-century warehouse (Lambert 1921, 62–72; Merrifield 1965, 91, 284).

The late 1950s and early 1960s saw the discovery of two Roman shipwrecks, one in Bermondsey (Marsden 1965), the other at Blackfriars (Marsden 1967). In 1962 Professor Grimes located the line of the pre-Roman river bank in Upper Thames Street (Grimes 1968, 57–64), while Ralph Merrifield's major treatise on Roman London, which included a discussion and gazetteer of waterfront features, appeared in 1965 (Merrifield 1965).

The majority of this work, although significant, was based primarily on observations of workmen digging foundations and sewer trenches rather than on scientifically conducted archaeological work. Prior to 1947 there was no provision for the controlled excavation of sites threatened with redevelopment. However, careful observation of building works could and occasionally did provide useful general information in the days when foundations were all dug by hand. For example, part of a bath-house was found near Pudding Lane in 1832, although the exact position was not recorded. The introduction of powerful machinery onto building sites meant that the archaeological deposits could be destroyed at a much greater speed, and casual observation was no longer a viable or safe method of collecting data.

The growing concern for the wholesale destruction of archaeological sites led to the establishment

5 *Salvage archaeology: recording what's left of a Roman timber quay ripped up by machines while a new office block rises in the background. Once the digging of new foundations has begun, only the briefest record can be made of the ancient structures destroyed.*

6 *Working on a controlled excavation conducted in advance of imminent development produces a much clearer picture of the ancient harbour structures. Cleaning up the fragile remains of a burnt timber floor in a waterfront warehouse means that a detailed photographic record can be made. Note the industrial cleaner. For the result, see Plate 1.*

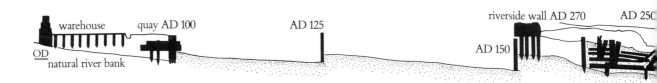

N

Thames Street

warehouse   quay AD 100   AD 125   riverside wall AD 270   AD 25(

AD 150

OD
natural river bank

7 *How London's waterfront advanced from the
first century* AD *to the present day: a simplified
north-south section across a 100m stratigraphic
sequence, with approximate dates.*

of an archaeological rescue unit in London, with
waterfront excavation a major priority (Biddle *et al*
1973, 4.14). From 1973 to 1983 knowledge of the
Roman harbour was revolutionised when modern
excavation techniques were finally brought to bear
upon the waterfront. A full-time team of excavators – often with volunteer support – examined
twelve major sites in this important decade.

As a result of all this work, it is now known that
reclamation or extension on the north bank of the
Thames from the first to the fifteenth centuries
advanced the line of the waterfront up to 100m
southwards, so that most of the Roman harbour lies
not below the buildings on the present-day waterfront, but partially beneath Thames Street, and
particularly north of it (Fig. 7).

The archaeological deposits have therefore accumulated in two directions simultaneously, both
upwards and southwards. The stratigraphic sequence of horizontally-bedded building debris and
surfaces is up to 4m thick, while the stratigraphic
sequence of waterfront extensions is over 100m
wide, surely one of the most deeply stratified sites
ever encountered. It is now standard practice to
attempt to excavate urban sites by removing the
deposits and features in the reverse order of that in
which they were laid (Barker 1977). In other
words, all the modern and post-medieval features
are removed before the medieval levels are recorded and excavated, and the Roman levels revealed.
In this way, as complete a plan as possible is
obtained for every building or phase of activity

represented on the site. Such a record is more
detailed and more reliable – and therefore ultimately more valuable – than the incomplete
drawings of sections cut at arbitrary points through
that sequence, which was all too often the best that
could be achieved working with earlier methodologies. Ideally, therefore, to excavate the London
waterfront, a long line of excavators should be
lined up on the present-day quayside and work
should progress downwards and northwards until
the natural riverbank was reached.

The procedure adopted in practice diverged
considerably from the ideal, since the excavation
programme was forced to keep pace with an
unprecedented rate of redevelopment. It was urban renewal rather than academic desirability
which dictated where, when and what might be
excavated. Within these severe constraints and
assuming financial support was made available
(which was not always the case), the only element
of selection was not which site to dig but which part
of an available site could be excavated in detail with
whatever resources were available. The siting of a
trench was itself determined by a variety of non-
academic factors such as the proximity of modern
foundations and roads, and the piling plan of the
proposed building.

Nevertheless, an attempt was made to mount an
archaeological excavation on part of every threatened waterfront site after (or during) demolition,
but before the subsequent redevelopment programme started. This has the advantage of ensur-
ing that at least part of the archaeological sequence
is recorded in the relative calm of a controlled
scientific excavation (Fig. 6). The timing of the

18

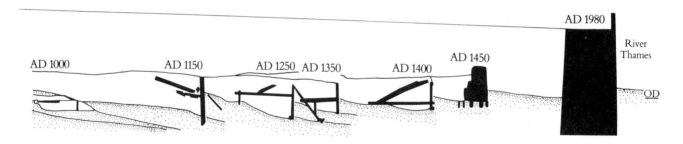

AD 1000 AD 1150 AD 1250 AD 1350 AD 1400 AD 1450 AD 1980

River Thames

OD

work on the main sites considered in this book was not, therefore, confined to the warm, dry summer months, but was designed to fit in with the demanding schedules of the development as a whole. All the time available on site was spent in carefully recording as much data as possible, the detailed evaluation of which was left until all the evidence collected was brought together during the compilation of the archive reports. Over 6000 features were identified and individually described on context-record sheets. Many were drawn at a scale of 1:20 on plans related to the site grid, and their absolute level in relation to Ordnance Datum (see p. 79) was measured. Sections and elevations were also drawn up, usually at a scale of 1:10 and an extensive photographic record in both black and white and colour was made. Thousands of potsherds and other artefacts were recovered and processed, together with over 300 environmental and dendrochronological samples.

This time-consuming work is labour-intensive and therefore expensive. Initially professional excavation staff were funded by the Department of the Environment, but, since 1979, the developers of the sites have made generous financial provision for the essential recording to be conducted by professional archaeologists. With the knowledge gained from the main excavation a smaller team of excavators would subsequently monitor the developers' large-scale earth-moving operations over the rest of the site. It must be stressed that evidence collected on such 'watching briefs' is not wholly reliable, since in these circumstances accurate measurement is rarely possible. Nevertheless, provided the observations can be related to data

recorded on controlled excavations, then a wide area can be covered at a fraction of the cost required to mount the initial investigation. A happy combination of these approaches is found on the Miles Lane site. The archaeological potential of the area was demonstrated in 1920 when part of a major Roman timber structure and a masonry building were observed during foundation preparation (Lambert 1921). Fifty years later a controlled archaeological excavation on the site established the level, position and date of these features, while the subsequent watching brief traced the Roman waterfront structure for a breathtaking 60m westwards (Fig. 5).

The Museum's commitment to extensive waterfront excavation has sampled the evidence of life in several parts of the Roman, Saxon, and medieval harbour from sites that would otherwise have been destroyed forever without record. The principal Roman discoveries include, on the northern side of Thames Street, the natural river bank and first-century quay structures at St James Garlickhithe (Dyson and Schofield 1981, 39, pl. 10), Miles Lane (Miller 1982) and on both sides of Pudding Lane (Milne 1982; Bateman and Milne 1983). Parts of riverside defensive walls were located under Thames Street itself at Baynards Castle (Hill et al 1980), New Fresh Wharf and within the precincts of the Tower of London (Parnell 1977; 1980; 1982), while just south of Thames Street substantial sections of second- and third-century quays were recorded on the Custom House (Tatton-Brown 1974), St Magnus House (Schofield and Miller 1976) and Billingsgate Lorry Park sites (Roskams forthcoming).

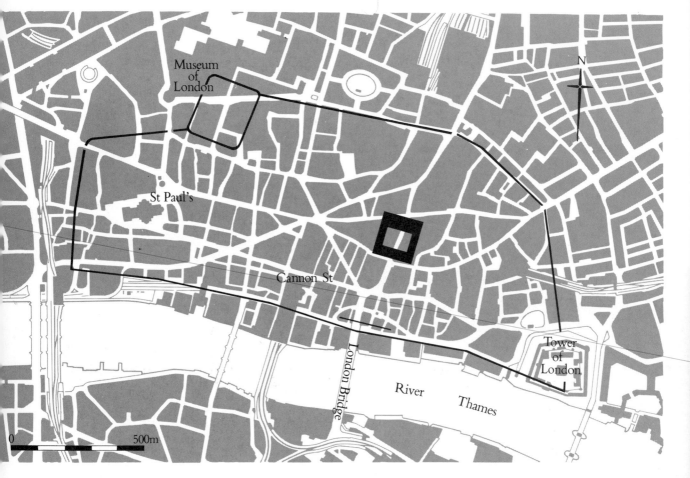

8 *Modern streets and bridges in London shown in relation to the Roman forum and City wall. The harbour excavations were close to London Bridge: see Fig. 9.*

The study area

The pattern of waterfront development presented here not only contributes substantially to the early history of London, but also provides one of the most detailed studies of a provincial Roman harbour complex yet compiled. Like most major urban archaeological studies, it is not the result of just one prestigious excavation, but the bringing together of information from several sites examined in a variety of ways over many years. The study area discussed in this book measures 270m east-west and over 150m north-south, centred on the present-day abutment of London Bridge, and extending both north and south of Thames Street

(Fig. 8). It is principally concerned with the work on the Miles Lane, Pudding Lane and Peninsular House sites recorded between 1979 and 1982, although the results of sites investigated from 1973–8 at St Magnus House, Billingsgate Buildings and Seal House are also considered, as are more recent excavations such as those at Billingsgate Lorry Park.

The piecemeal chronology of archaeological investigation is shown on Fig. 9 where the sites are numbered in the order in which controlled excavation began. Although this particular area accounts for only 15 per cent of the City waterfront, it merits intensive study since it can be shown to lie at the heart of the ancient harbour.

In Chapter 2, an interpretation of the Roman activity represented on the waterfront is summarised. It is suggested that the development spans the period from the first to the fifth century AD, and evidence for this dating is discussed in Chapter 3. Later chapters examine aspects of the

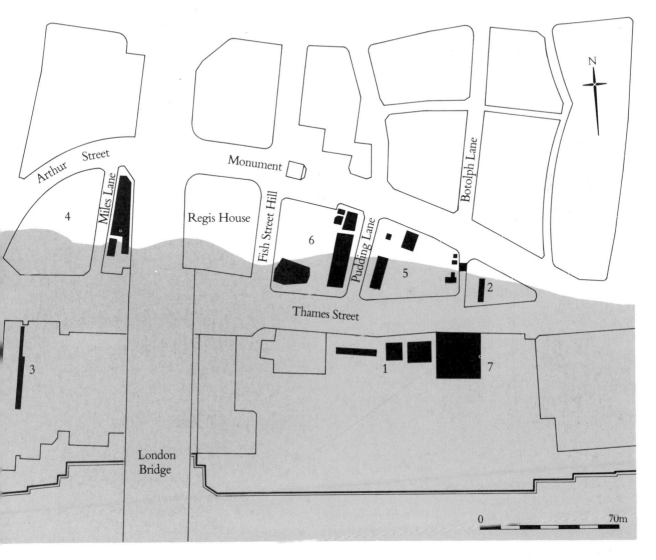

9 *Recent archaeological excavations in the study area of London's Roman harbour numbered in the order in which work commenced, reflecting the haphazard progress of redevelopment.*
1 St Magnus House 2 Billingsgate Buildings
3 Seal House 4 Miles Lane 5 Peninsular House
6 Pudding Lane 7 Billingsgate Lorry Park.
Tone shows northern extent of mid-first-century river at high tide. The natural river bank and the earliest harbour works were discovered 100m north of the present-day Thames.

structural, environmental and finds analysis in greater detail, while implications for the study of London as a whole are considered in the final chapter.

The relatively modest size of the warehouses and of the quayside commercial zone itself, the nature of the traffic handled in the harbour, the type of craft it could have accommodated and the pattern of waterfront development are all evaluated, necessitating a critical reappraisal of the role of this Roman port.

CHAPTER 2

GROWTH OF A ROMAN HARBOUR

The pattern of waterfront activity which is presented here traces the growth of the Roman harbour from the mid-first century, through the second and into the early third century (a period marked by substantial expansion), examines the changing fortunes of life in the fourth century, and finally considers the evidence for the demise of urban activity by the fifth century. Most of the information was recorded on the sites either side of Miles Lane, to the west of London Bridge, where the development of Buildings A–F was traced (Fig. 12) and the excavations either side of Pudding Lane, to the east of the Bridge, where Buildings 1 to 9 were recorded (Fig. 13).

The prehistoric riverbank

It is clear that the north bank of the Thames in the area was drastically altered by Roman terracing, embanking and waterfront extension. So great was the change that it proved difficult to find the immediately pre-Roman land surface undisturbed. However, evidence of an even earlier landscape was exposed on one site (Peninsular House, Area D), where truncated deposits which had accumulated in a small marsh over 9000 years ago were revealed directly beneath a Roman building platform laid several millennia later (Fig. 11). A provisional examination by Dr Scaife of the pollen from the ancient peats provides a fascinating glimpse into the prehistoric environment of the waterfront. In this period, shortly after the glaciers had retreated from England, the climate was cooler and drier than it is today. Generally, the Thames valley seems to have been thickly wooded with pine trees, and some birch. In the hillside, where the abutment for the first London Bridge was to be built more than 7000 years later, there was a badly-drained depression several metres across. This marshy ground was shaded by willows and was thick with sedges and grasses interspersed with wild flowers such as marsh marigold, mint, meadow sweet, loosestrife, water plantain, buttercups

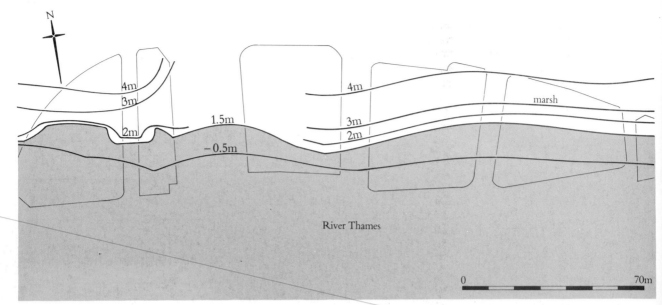

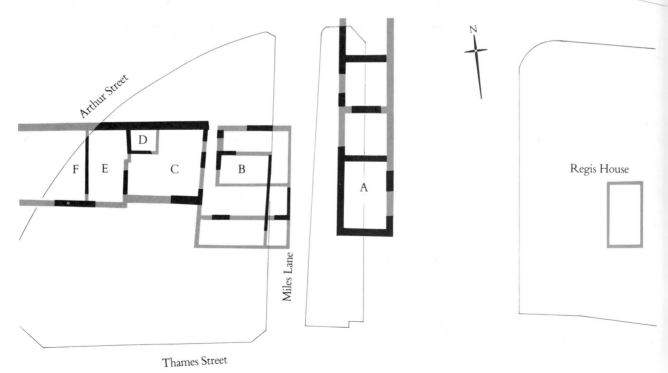

11 *Plan of study area showing contours and extent of river at high tide (toned) in first century* AD, *in relation to modern street plan. Compare Figs. 8 and 9. Note position of Mesolithic marsh.*

12 *The recent controlled excavations and observations on the Miles Lane sites to the west of London Bridge revealed the plans of Buildings A to F. Conjectured wall lines toned.*

and docks. However, it has been suggested that in this period the main channel of the River Thames itself followed a course which was *c*3km south of the present-day City. This Thames channel subsequently migrated northwards in several stages, but may not have adopted its present position in the London area until after 500 BC and possibly not much earlier than the Roman occupation (Nunn 1983, fig. 8).

Although knowledge of the environment in the early first century AD is less specific, the main elements of the natural topography have been established, as the schematic representation of the natural contours on Fig. 11 shows. The data for this were compiled from controlled excavations, the less reliable observations of deposits exposed during contractors' site work, the results of bore hole surveys, and, on the areas not available for study, simple guesswork.

The gradient of the hillside slopes downwards from + 4m OD, and a stream valley was found in the centre of the area. The line of the 1.5m contour is of

13 *Multi-period plan of recent excavations on the Pudding Lane sites to the east of London Bridge, showing the superimposed plans of Buildings 1 to 9. Conjectured wall lines toned.*

especial importance since it marks the point above which the Roman River Thames was not expected to rise. The present-day river bank is over 100m to the south. (A detailed assessment of the first-century river is made in Chapter 7.)

Mid-first century

Deposits of London Clay, sands and gravels were exposed on the foreshore, bank and hillside, and the earliest Roman activity on the site included pits presumably dug to extract this material. The largest of the quarries was 11m by 8m. All were clearly Roman rather than prehistoric features, and some had been cut on the foreshore from the level of Ordnance Datum, over 1m below the contemporary high tide. This implies that the Roman Thames must have been tidal at this point, that is to say it must have receded temporarily below the level at which the quarries were cut. Fig. 14a shows the river at low tide, leaving the quarries exposed. Other features on the foreshore which may also have been of mid-first-century date include various pile rows; a flint and chalk spread perhaps marking an access point, and evidence of attempts at protecting the banks and containing the river, such as a modest gravel embankment strengthened with piles, and a post and plank facing or revet-

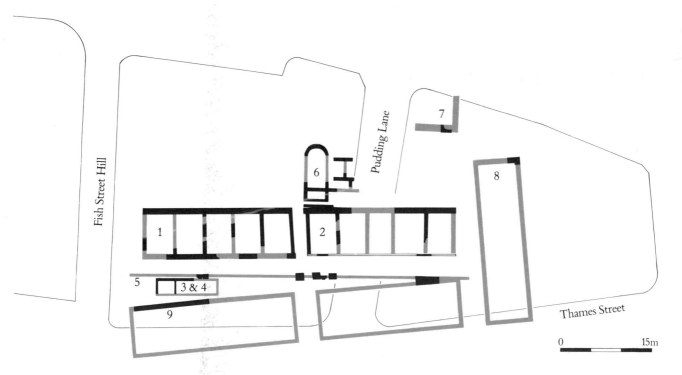

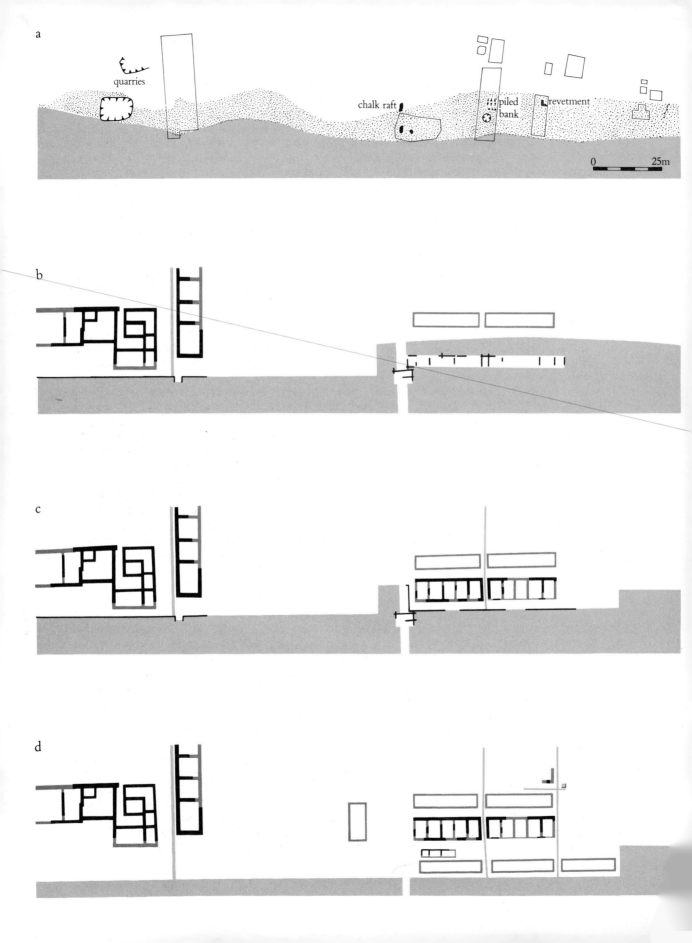

a

quarries

chalk raft

piled
bank

revetment

0   25m

b

c

d

ment. In sum, the foreshore saw considerable and varied activity in the early decades of Roman occupation, although it was of a quite different character from that which followed.

Late first century

By the late first century the area had been transformed, but the development in the west contrasted significantly with that in the east (Fig. 14b). The line of the waterfront had been advanced by up to 15m with the erection of a vast artificial terrace retained by a framework of braced timber baulks stacked horizontally one upon another. With the exception of a small jetty which extended out into the river at one point, this massive engineering project produced a uniform frontage with a surface raised over 2m above flood level, on which buildings were laid out. At least six buildings have been identified (Fig. 12), and these have been labelled Buildings A–F by the excavator (Miller 1982). The western group, Buildings B–F, extended southwards from a 1.5m wide masonry wall which formed the northern limit of the waterfront terrace and revetted the southern limit of a higher terrace. Robber trenches marked the position of all the other walls of Buildings B and C, but Buildings D–F incorporated tile walls up to 0.6m wide laid over a brickearth slab with no other foundation. At the eastern edge of this development was a gravel yard or street through which the stream was canalised in a timber-revetted channel. To the east of that was a massive masonry-walled building (Building A) which had been erected in the mouth of the infilled stream valley. It was aligned north-south, was 9m wide and was at least 35m long (Fig. 15).

14 *Early Roman development in the study area.*

a *Mid-first-century features on stippled foreshore below the 1.5m contour (see Fig. 11) with river at low tide shown toned.*

b *Late first-century Buildings A to F to west of bridge (see Fig. 12); landing stage to east with conjectured timber warehouses to north.*

c *By AD 100, landing stage east of bridge replaced by infilled quay and masonry horrea, Buildings 1 and 2 (see Fig. 13).*

d *Early second-century extension. To west of bridge, note position of Regis House samian store destroyed in cAD 130 fire; to east note addition of Building 4, Building 7 near which fish sauce was prepared, and position of conjectured warehouses in south.*

Controlled excavation of the eastern group of sites produced a quite different pattern. Substantial traces of à timber landing stage were found, perhaps extending for as much as 57m east-west. The braced front wall comprised horizontally stacked timber baulks similar to those used in the extension in the west, but, unlike the latter structure, it had not been infilled. Instead it functioned as a substantial open framework, presumably supporting timber decking, built out into the river over the foreshore to facilitate the movement of men and merchandise from ship to shore. Gangways would have been required to gain access from bank to landing stage; these may have been supported at the landward end by features such as the substantial 1.5m wide masonry wall which revetted the made ground to the north.

The foreshore beneath the landing stage was littered with broken pottery (Fig. 36), a thick deposit of oyster shells and, in one area, a quantity of wood shavings representing *in situ* timber working. This was of especial interest since some of the species present were identified by V. Straker as non-native softwoods. However, imported barrel fragments were also identified in these deposits, suggesting that such containers were being broken up and recycled on the waterfront.

A timber box structure 7m by 5m was partially recorded on the foreshore at the south west corner of the landing-stage, and this has been interpreted as part of a Roman bridge foundation (see Chapter 5). The decking of the bridge itself would have been supported on a series of such pier-bases, spanning the river.

In contrast to the development in the west, which may have been predominantly residential, the location of the bridge with a landing-stage downstream of it suggests that the eastern side of the area was specifically designed to accommodate river traffic. Whatever buildings occupied the terrace to the north of the landing-stage were probably timber rather than masonry since all trace of them was removed by later activity. It could be argued that storage buildings, or *horrea* (see Chapter 6), may initially have been erected there (Fig. 14b).

Upstream of the bridge, no major storage buildings have as yet been recognised in plan. However, a similar pattern of masonry structures laid out over an artificial waterfront terrace has been traced to the mouth of the Walbrook stream, over 200m to the west. The western end of this massive development is perhaps marked by the waterfront struc-

15 *The tile and masonry west wall of Building* A *With 2 × 100mm scale, sitting on its substantial off-set foundation.*

ture found near St James Garlickhithe (Dyson and Schofield 1981, 39) – some 500m west of London Bridge – from which timbers felled in cAD 70–80 were recovered. It is suggested that a market complex was also built at this date on the crest of the hill overlooking the harbour and bridge (Chapter 6).

By the end of the first century, the landing stage had collapsed or been dismantled. An artificial terrace at $c+2$m OD, revetted by a braced timber wall similar to that described to the west, was laid out over the foreshore (Figs. 14c, 38, Pls. 1, 4b) and incorporated several of the timbers from the earlier staging. This timber quay extended c80m east-west, beyond which, to the east, only pile and plank revetments were observed, although a more substantial structure of a similar date was recorded some 300m further to the east on the Custom House site (Tatton-Brown 1974; Fletcher 1982).

Within the study area, two ranges of open-fronted five-bay buildings were erected over the newly-won land as an integral part of the development (Pl. 5a; Buildings 1 and 2 on Figs. 13, 14c). They are interpreted as storage buildings to which the general latin term *horrea* may be applied (see Chapter 6). The position of these buildings emphasises once again the commercial nature of this particular area. Higher up the hillside, a substantial timber and gravel raft formed a platform upon which another building was constructed, of which a masonry wall fragment was found (Building 7, Figs. 13, 14d). Nearby, a complex of drains and a timber-lined tank, probably used in the processing of fish by-products, had been established (see Chapter 8). All these features are thought to form part of the same general redevelopment scheme. No major changes were recorded in the building layout to the west of the bridge in this phase.

Early second century

However, some time in the early second century, the timber floor of Building B (Figs. 12 and 14d) was badly burnt, as were the timber elements in an associated timber raft. The dumps which sealed this destruction horizon were contemporary with the replacement of the drain next to Building A. This masonry building was also affected by the fire, and the walls of the northernmost rooms were completely rebuilt with brick set in pink *opus signinum*. Subsequently, the waterfront was again advanced, this time by at least 15m (Fig. 14d). The revetment forming the face of the new artificial river bank was glimpsed at the extreme southern edge of one site, but elsewhere lay beyond the limit of excavation beneath Thames Street itself. However, the material tipped in the area between the old and the new frontages was observed and parts of buildings, laid out over the newly-won land, were recorded. To the west of the bridge, the floor of Building B was extended, implying that the southern wall was now founded on the highest surviving member of the old quay.

To the east, on the Pudding Lane site, two superimposed buildings erected in front of the masonry horrea (Building 1) had mud brick walls laced with timber elements (Buildings 3 and 4, Figs. 14d and 16). Once again, the uppermost surviving member of the old quay was used as a foundation, but here it supported the north wall. A massive dump of fire-damaged mud-brick debris which had been spread out over the area after a

serious fire implies that an additional range of such buildings had been erected directly overlooking the river. Large fragments of painted wallplaster were found with the debris, which could imply that some of the buildings were domestic dwellings, although Roman commercial buildings such as *macella* are also known to have been decorated in that way (de Ruyt 1983, 307–10). However, there is evidence to show that waterfront storage buildings were also destroyed. For example, a similar debris deposit was recorded in the 1920s at Regis House (Fig. 9) immediately west of London Bridge, and was associated with an extensive collection of fire-blackened samian ware, a common type of imported Roman pottery which normally has a glossy red finish. A study of this remarkable concentration of vessels led to the conclusion that the warehouse in which the pottery had been stored occupied a site in the vicinity at the time of the fire (Marsh 1981, 221–4). A deposit of carbonised grain was also found mixed with the fire debris in the area to the east of the bridge. After a detailed analysis of the deposit, Vanessa Straker was able to suggest that it represented the type of processed product 'that would usually be consigned to a bulk store . . . or shop for sale' (Straker 1984, 327).

Although considerable damage was caused by these fires – which may not represent a single event – they seem to have been confined to the central area of the harbour. For example, the timber floor in the western bays of the masonry horrea (Pl. 5, Building 2) were so badly burnt that they were reduced to charcoal, whereas the planking in the more easterly bays was untouched by the fire. The buildings on the eastern and western sides of the study area were not affected, nor was there any trace of fire damage on the higher terrace to the north (Buildings 7 and 8).

Mid- to late second century

The aftermath of the fire saw a major reorganisation of the area (Fig. 17a). The line of the contemporary timber-revetted waterfront was established some 25m south of the late first-century quay. A section of it was cursorily observed at the St Magnus House site (Miller *et al*, forthcoming), and in more detail at the Custom House site (Tatton-Brown 1974). The orientation of this frontage seems to have differed from the previous one, and this difference is reflected in the alignment of some fire-resistant masonry structures established in the vicinity. One of these buildings probably ran north-south (Building 8,

16 *Part of Building 4, looking south. Its north and west walls have burned down, exposing the opus signinum floor, with 0.5m scale. Note column base in adjoining room.*

Figs. 13, 17a), since it occupied a confined space in the east between other buildings and a metalled yard or road. A range of buildings to the south was represented solely by fragments of the north wall (Building 9, Figs. 13 and 17a), but these or a structure close to them were probably used to store samian pottery. The evidence for this is a large concentration of samian vessels, presumably derived from the clearance of an adjacent storehouse, which was found in association with a quay built in the early third century (Miller *et al*, forthcoming).

To the north, the modifications to the plan of at least one of the five-bay masonry buildings suggest that it was now primarily a shop rather than a store (see Chapter 6). This would seem to be a response to the now increased distance between the quay front and the buildings, and implies that the storage role formerly played by them was taken over by the structures erected to the south. The harbour area was not the only part of Roman London which expanded dramatically in this period. By the mid-second century, it has been argued, a massive forum complex had been built *c*300m to the north, which could also imply an increase in commercial activity (Marsden 1980, 98–103).

Just to the north, overlooking the waterfront market area, was an elegant masonry building laid out over a terrace now cleared of the timber structures thought to have occupied it previously (Building 6, Figs. 13 and 17a). Only the western wing was recorded, but, since this incorporated a drainage system linked to a substantial latrine and an apsidal-ended plunge bath with white tessellated walls, it is suggested that a small inn rather than a private dwelling may be represented (Pl. 5b; see Chapter 11).

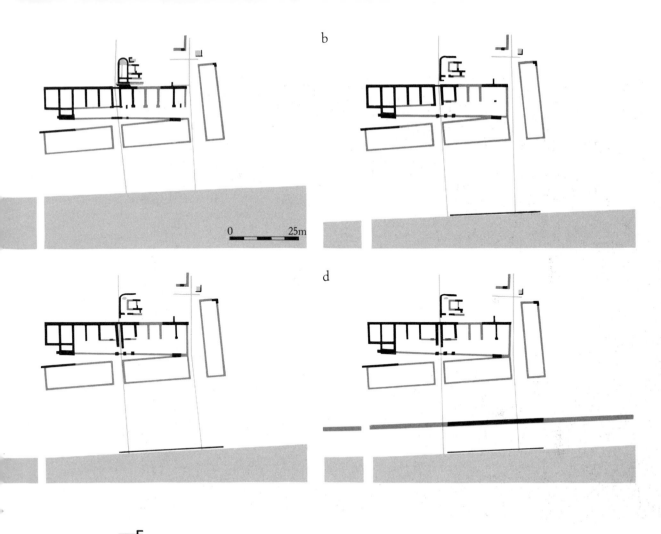

17 *Second- to fourth-century development in the eastern half of study area on the Pudding Lane sites. Compare Fig. 13.*

a *Post-fire development. By late second century, waterfront advanced again. Bath wing of Building 6, a small inn, and masonry Buildings 8 and 9 introduced.*

b *Early third century. The final waterfront advance saw drains reset and modifications to Buildings 1, 2 and 6.*

c *Mid-third-century modifications.*

d *Mid-fourth century. Some of the buildings are partially dismantled. To south is riverside defensive wall built in the late third century.*

e *Late fourth-century revival. Drains infilled, Building 6 rebuilt, Building 5 introduced.*

To the west of the bridge a rather different picture emerges at the end of the second century, by which time most of the walls of Buildings B, C, D and E had been dismantled and sealed beneath brickearth and mortar dumps. Only Building A, with its main drain re-set for a third time, and the southern extension of Building B seem to be in use at this stage.

Third century

The final advance of the Roman waterfront was effected in the early third century, and a substantial section of this timber quay was recorded to the south of Thames Street on the St Magnus House (Miller and Schofield 1976; Miller *et al*, forthcoming), and Billingsgate Lorry Park sites (Fig. 9). By that date, an artificial terrace over 50m wide had been created along part of the harbour. Structures of a similar date and position were recorded at the Seal House and Swan Lane sites just to the west of the bridge, but the eastern limit of this latest extension has not been established, although it certainly did not extend as far east as the Custom House site.

To the west of the bridge the drain next to Building A was infilled and not replaced, and the ground surface raised over it. The floors in Building A were made up by 0.5–0.7m, and a new doorway cut in the west wall gave access from the southern room to a covered area extending up to 18m to the south, defined by postholes and beaten clay floors which were resurfaced five times. Building B was also extended riverwards, and the robber foundations of Buildings E and F seem to have been replaced by new clay and brickearth footings, although Buildings C and D were not rebuilt. However, the remains of these buildings were all ultimately covered by deposits of dark grey silt containing third- and fourth-century pottery. Building A seems to have survived the longest, and here floors containing sherds of third-century pottery were cut by stakeholes marking the position of partitions, which were sealed by fire debris. Unfortunately, this horizon was cut by the modern cellar floor so the fate of the building is not known. Nevertheless, it is suggested that it certainly continued in use throughout the third century, and presumably into the fourth.

East of the bridge, the plan of both the range of shops and the possible inn were also changed significantly after the early third-century advance, and take on the form of more standard domestic dwellings (Fig. 17b). In the former inn the bath and the latrine were infilled and new corridors and rooms were laid out, one of which had a mosaic floor. Each bay in the building to the south was developed independently from this point onwards, suggesting that the shell of the former warehouse had now been divided up into separate apartments. The implication is, once again, that the commercial activity had moved south in step with the waterfront advance. This pattern was continued through the third century with modifications such as the introduction of a small bath into Building 6 (Fig. 17c).

Early to mid-fourth century

However, the relative prosperity and residential character of the development suggested by the previous plans did not continue without interruption, for the area seems to have taken on the appearance of a run-down, decaying urban site by the mid-fourth century (Fig. 17d). The evidence for the changes took different forms in different places. Part of Building 6 was demolished, and door posts were crudely dug through a mosaic floor to secure part of the sub-divided building, while irregular trenches recorded in what had been the southern range of rooms suggest some activity quite inconsistent with their former use. A similar series of irregular pits and trenches was found elsewhere on the site and again no specific interpretation can be offered other than that of a phase of activity completely different from the preceding one is represented.

The slags and ash found near a hearth recorded in Building 2 could suggest that some sort of industrial process may have been conducted there. To the north, the area associated with fish processing fell into disuse, and was covered by a thick layer of mud, while the adjacent masonry building was left standing derelict.

Some reasons for this decline in activity are considered in Chapter 12, and all that need be noted in this summary is a possible effect of the building of a riverside defensive wall, part of which was erected in the late third century (Sheldon and Tyers 1984) some 7m north of the contemporary quay front. This substantial structure effectively separated the commercial quayside harbour area from the rest of the town, and would have presented a considerable physical obstacle to traffic on the waterfront. How important a factor this may have been in the decline of activity in the hinterland is debatable. What seems unquestionable is that there were no major advances on the waterfront itself in the century and a half of Roman occupation which followed the wall's construction, a significant hiatus given the regularity of the extensions in the previous 200 years.

Late fourth century

The story does not end there, however, for there is a growing body of evidence from the St Peters Hill site in the west (Williams 1982) to the Roman building found in the Tower of London in the east (Butcher 1982, 100–5), not only for continued occupation on the waterfront in the late fourth century, but for a positive revival. In the study area, this is seen most vividly in the development of Building 6, the complete rebuilding of which incorporated rooms heated by hypocausts and a small bath (Fig. 17e). This major development overlay deposits containing coins dated to cAD 375 (see Chapter 3).

To the south, the eastern range of buildings which had started life as a waterfront warehouse 300 years earlier, continued to be occupied at this date, as the sequence of internal surfaces and features shows. However, the main drain which ran north-south between Buildings 1 and 2 (an integral part of the initial and subsequent layout of the area) was infilled and not replaced. Spanning its former course was a line of T-shaped tiled plinths thought to mark the north wall of an open-sided building, perhaps with a portico (Building 5, Figs. 13, 17e). Other signs of this short-lived revival were seen in the north of the area, where the derelict buildings were pulled down and the ground surface levelled up in a systematic fashion.

Although much of this important late Roman material was truncated, some deposits were found to be sealed *in situ* by dark grey silts, or by waterlaid silts associated with the blocking of the drainage system, which must mark the effective end of urban occupation in the harbour area, presumably in the early fifth century. However, a short sequence of features was recorded between the horizons representing the late Roman revival and the demise of waterfront occupation. The most notable features were a possible sunken-floored building laid out within the shell of Building 2, and some internal floors or hearths. Taken together, this could suggest a period of activity of no more than 100 years, although the latest surfaces may well have been eroded or subsequently truncated. Since the next phase of intensive occupation is of mid- to late Saxon date (Milne 1980), it now seems certain that this part of London did not survive as a recognisable urban settlement much beyond the fifth century.

This study of the Roman harbour has therefore traced the pattern of waterfront development for a period of some 400 years. Such a long and detailed occupation sequence is of considerable significance, not least because it contrasts markedly with the more contracted pattern recorded in London on sites away from the waterfront, the settlement of which often seems to have been abandoned by AD 200. Thus the development of the harbour can be seen to reflect the changing prosperity of the town as a whole: after almost two centuries of energetic expansion, Roman London shrank to a small community mainly on the waterfront. There is no evidence for urban settlement here in the sixth century.

DATING THE DEVELOPMENT

A relative chronology

The Roman levels examined in the study area were recorded in many different trenches and areas excavated over a ten year period. The pattern of development suggested in Chapter 2 is therefore a complex reconstruction involving the integration of the results from many separate excavations. The field record compiled for every trench was analysed and a sequence of activity suggested for each one. These formed the basis of the official archive reports, which are housed in the Museum of London library. These 'area sequences' together comprised the evidence for a number of phases of activity. These horizons were not assigned *absolute dates* initially, although their relative chronology, established by stratigraphic analysis, was known, ie A was earlier then B; C was later than B, etc.

In order to produce an overall picture of waterfront development, these 'area sequences' had to be integrated and a 'master sequence' established. To do this, features found in different trenches but which were thought to represent the same phase of activity would have to be correlated. Fortunately, parts of a number of major features such as the timber quay, the warehouse buildings and the main north-south drain were recorded in several separate excavations, conveniently providing a number of fixed points at which otherwise discrete 'area sequences' came together. In this way, it was possible to suggest not only that a particular readily identifiable phase of construction was common to, say, three separate 'area sequences', but that features in the succeeding and preceding phases which are less obviously related, could also represent broadly contemporary activity. (These phases are shown in brackets in Fig. 18.)

To the east of the bridge, the main elements in the 'master sequence' (shown in block capitals in Fig. 18) are:

the landing stage, the construction of which defined an earlier group of otherwise unrelated features;

the infilled eastern quay, the construction of which was later than the landing stage and bridge pier base, contemporary with the warehouse buildings (Buildings 1 and 2) but earlier than the bath-house (Building 6);

the major fire debris horizon, which was later than the waterfront advance superseding the eastern quay mentioned above;

the resetting of the main drain which was contemporary with developments in both Buildings 2 and 6, and was probably contemporary with the latest waterfront advance recorded south of Thames Street;

the deliberate infilling of the main drain;

the horizon of dark grey silts which sealed the uppermost layers of the occupation sequence, where they survived intact.

This framework provides a relative chronology for the development of the waterfront in the study area, based on direct and indirect stratigraphic relationships. At this stage, the evidence on which the 'absolute dating' of the published sequence rests can be considered, and this is summarised in Fig. 18. For each phase of activity represented, the material for which a date range can be determined was brought together. After careful analysis, it was possible to suggest dates for most of the phases, and these are usually expressed to the nearest quarter century rather than to a specific year. Attempts at dating most of the activity represented more closely, for example to the decade, applies more weight to the dating evidence than it can reasonably bear. Although every effort should be made to establish as close a date as possible, the unsupportably precise dating of archaeological features is at best misleading and at worst wrong.

Several phases of the stratigraphic sequence recorded on the Miles Lane site to the west of London Bridge were also dated (Fig. 19). They included:

Phase	Dendrochronology	Coins	Pottery	Suggested date
(pre-landing stage)	after 59 before 74			M1
LANDING STAGE	after 69 before 91			M–L1
(pre-E quay)	after 78 before 118	41		M–L1
E QUAY	after 86 before 106	43–60	50–80	L1
(pre-fire)	after 93		100–120	E–M2
FIRE DEBRIS			140–180	M–L2
(post-fire)		141		L2–E3
RESET DRAIN		81–96	200–240	E3
(post reset drain deposits)		367–375	250–350	M3–L4
INFILLED DRAIN		364–367	350+	L4
(pre-grey silt horizon)		348–351	350+	L4–E5
GREY SILT HORIZON		330–335	350+	E–M5

18 *Summary of dating evidence for the eastern quay sites near Pudding Lane.*

the foreshore features, terracing and terrace walls which are demonstrably earlier than the construction of the western quay;

the western quay itself, the establishment of which was broadly contemporary with the initial laying out of Buildings A–F, but stratigraphically earlier than the construction of Drain 1;

the infill of Drain 1, its replacement by Drain 2 and the revetment extension;

the infill of Drain 2 and its replacement by Drain 3;

the infill of Drain 3 and the overlying dumping which was contemporary with substantial resurfacing within Building A;

later surfaces and features within Building A which represent activity contemporary with an accumulation of dark grey silts over the remains of Buildings C–F.

Once the sequences recorded on the eastern and western groups of waterfront sites had been dated, they could be integrated, and the results are shown in Chapter 2.

Absolute dating, ie a historical time-scale, was imposed upon the London waterfront sequence only after the stratigraphic assessment of the field record had been integrated with an analysis of the pottery, dendrochronological samples, and coins. Each of the three studies contributed positively to the pattern suggested in the right-hand column of Figs. 18 and 19, although no one study on its own was able to support the entire framework. The results could not always be taken at face value, but needed to be assessed in the light of the stratigraphic evidence before a date for the development represented could be proposed. For example, it is argued on stratigraphic grounds that

Phase	Dendrochronology	Coins	Pottery	Suggested date
(pre-W QUAY)	after 13			M1
W QUAY	after 45	41–54		
BUILDINGS A–F	after 67 before 79			
DRAIN 1	after 47 before 89			M–L1
DRAIN 1 INFILLED			70–100	
DRAIN 2	after 51		100–120	
REVETMENT EXTENSION	after 61	71–8	100–120	E2
DRAIN 2 INFILLED			150–200	
DRAIN 3				M–L2
DRAIN 3 INFILLED			200–240	
DUMPS OVER DRAIN			150–200	E3
BUILDING A			200–250	
GREY SILTS OVER BUILDINGS				
B–F			250–350	M3–L4

19 *Summary of dating evidence for the western quay sites near Miles Lane.*

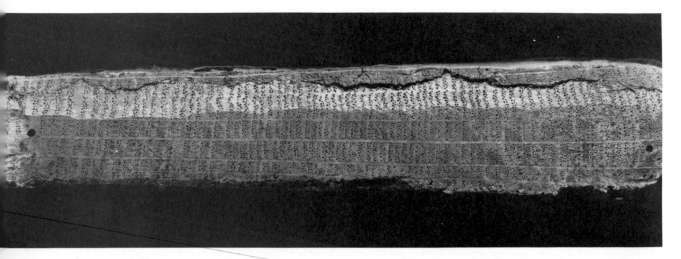

20 *Sample cut from an ancient London waterfront timber showing some 80 annual growth rings. Once the ring widths have been measured and the ensuing pattern matched with a master chronology, the dendrochronologist can suggest a felling date for the timber.*

the grey silt horizon which sealed much of the Roman activity on the Pudding Lane site was laid in the fifth century, even though the deposits themselves only contained early fourth-century coins and late fourth-century pottery. Since the analysis of the coins, dendrochronological samples and the pottery represent three contrasting methodologies which have produced results of varying reliability; each will be considered in turn.

Dendrochronology

Dendrochronology is the science of dating wood, based on the simple principle that trees such as oak grow a new layer every year during the spring and summer (Fig. 20). Seen in a tree's cross section, these layers appear as the more or less concentric circles familiarly known as tree-rings: an 82-year-old tree will have 82 rings. The *width* of each individual ring is determined by the environmental conditions, such as rainfall, prevalent during the growing season. Adverse conditions often result in the formation of noticeably narrower rings than those which form in more favourable years. A distinctive pattern of narrow and wide rings when measured and drawn up as a graph by the dendrochronologist is termed a chronology, and may be the result of averaging the ring widths pattern from several contemporary samples. The

chronology thus formed may be extended in either direction by the subsequent identification and matching of samples which partially overlap it. In this way, it is possible to provide *relative dating* for timbers from successive structures recorded on an excavation: for example, Structure A may be shown to contain timbers felled 17 years before those in Structure B, but 94 years before those in Structure C.

The *absolute dating* of structural or site chronologies depends primarily upon matching them with one of the dated reference chronologies from Germany, Ireland or Scotland (Pilcher *et al* 1984) which have been constructed from successively older tree-ring patterns starting with modern samples. The accuracy of the date derived from such an exercise depends upon the presence or absence of sapwood. If the sapwood is completely preserved up to the bark edge, then the exact year in which the tree was felled can be determined. This situation is rarely encountered in archaeological contexts, since most if not all of the sapwood was usually removed when the trunk was dressed during conversion into building timbers. However, if the junction of the heartwood and sapwood rings survives, ie the earliest sapwood is still identifiable, then a felling date can be suggested by estimating what the full complement of sapwood rings may have been. The number of sapwood rings is relatively constant: an oak tree over 50 years old is unlikely to have less than ten or more than 50 sapwood rings if it grew in the British Isles (Hillam *et al* forthcoming). If no sapwood survives at all, but the final ring of a sample can be dated, then the only possible estimation for the felling date of the tree is that it must have been at least ten years after that date.

In 1975, the Department of the Environment set up the Dendrochronological Laboratory at Sheffield University primarily to provide a dating service for archaeologists. Hundreds of waterlogged oak timbers from many sites in London and from all over England have been examined since then, resulting in the production of several discrete Roman, Saxon, medieval and post-medieval tree-ring sequences. Initially, neither the Roman nor the Saxon chronologies could be tied to specific years. However, by 1980 an absolutely-dated chronology spanning the years AD 404–1216 had been established (Hillam 1981). Attention was then turned to the 'floating' Roman sequences. Recent excavations in London had uncovered many Roman timbers, particularly at the waterfront sites. As early as 1976, ring sequences from the Seal House and St Magnus House sites were crossmatched to produce a 282-year floating chronology, to which sequences from Thames Street Tunnel and two inland sites at Milk Street and Watling Court were later added. A Roman London chronology was thus constructed by averaging the ring widths from the St Magnus House, Thames Street Tunnel and Watling Court samples. Using a computer program developed in Belfast, this chronology was compared with a curve from the Danube Valley area of South Germany (Becker 1981) and Hollstein's West German chronology, which stretched from 700 BC to AD 1975 (Hollstein 1980). A 461-year sequence spanning the period 252 BC to AD 209 was thus established (Hillam and Morgan 1981). This was subsequently extended to AD 255 (Sheldon and Tyers 1983) and then to AD 294 (Hillam, forthcoming).

Over 270 samples were sawn from the Roman timbers on the sites either side of Pudding Lane and Miles Lane, and half of them were successfully matched with the Roman London chronology. Felling dates were estimated for the samples on which sapwood survived, but unfortunately this was only 10 per cent of the total, an exceptionally low percentage. However, a date for the latest surviving tree ring is also shown for each structure on Figs. 18 and 19, and this provides a firm date before which the structure could not have been erected.

Analysis of the samples from the Pudding Lane sites (Fig. 21) suggests that the latest felling date for timber incorporated in:

a revetment erected on the foreshore (before the landing stage was built) was after AD 59 but before AD 74, possibly cAD 70;

the landing stage itself, after AD 69, but before AD 91, possibly cAD 80;

the bridge pier-base, after AD 78 but before AD 118, possibly cAD 85–90, since the feature is stratigraphically earlier than the eastern quay;

the eastern quay itself, after AD 86 but before AD 106, possibly cAD 90–5

the timber floor of Building 2, after AD 84 but before AD 124, possibly cAD 95, since the building was clearly erected in the same construction phase as the underlying quay.

A number of samples with no surviving sapwood from several other structures were also successfully matched. However, in no instance could a felling date be proposed (although it must obviously have been at least ten years later than the latest surviving ring), since the position of the outermost ring could not be estimated. For example, a post-and-plank revetment possibly erected before the landing stage was constructed after AD 39; the drains laid out after the eastern quay was initially extended could be dated later than AD 70, and a foundation raft on the hillside terrace to the north of the quay, after AD 34.

Even though it was not possible to date the erection of the major timber structures to a specific year, the dendrochronological analysis was able to resolve several other problems. For example, it showed that there was only a ten to fifteen year period between the erection of the landing stage and the succeeding quay structure, while the bridge pier-base (which is known to have been in position before the quay) was constructed shortly after the landing stage.

Another major attribute of dendrochronological work is that it enables close comparisons to be made between sites which are otherwise widely separated. This point is demonstrated by the analysis of the material from the Miles Lane site to the west of the bridge (Fig. 22). Although only four of the matched samples had any sapwood at all, it was nevertheless possible to suggest that the western quay complex with its associated buildings was laid out before AD 79. It can therefore be seen as an earlier development than the equivalent project to the east of the bridge, and would have been broadly contemporary with the landing stage structure found on the Pudding Lane site.

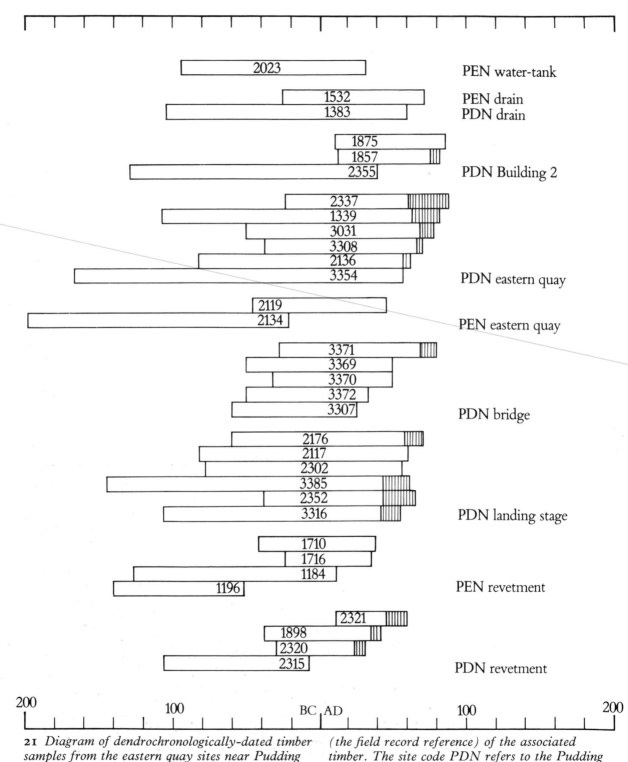

200   100   BC AD   100   200

21 *Diagram of dendrochronologically-dated timber samples from the eastern quay sites near Pudding Lane, with the extent of surviving sapwood shown hatched. Each sample carries the context number (the field record reference) of the associated timber. The site code PDN refers to the Pudding Lane site, PEN to the Peninsular House site (see Fig. 9).*

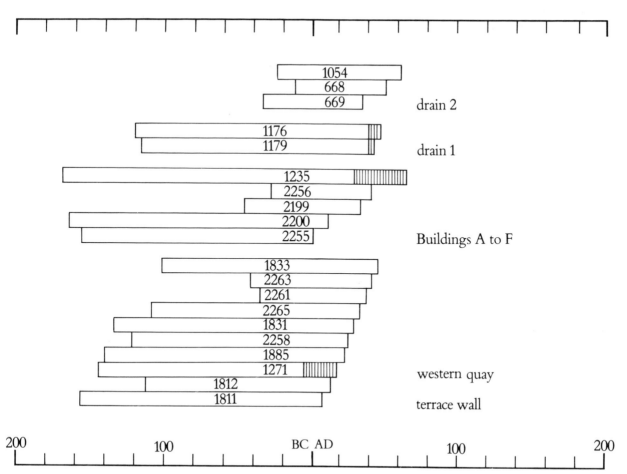

22 *Diagram of dendrochronologically-dated timber samples from the western quay sites near Miles Lane. Some of the timbers shown here and on the previous table were over 200 years old when felled.*

This summary has therefore demonstrated that dendrochronological analysis provided an exceptionally firm foundation for the Roman waterfront chronology by showing that none of the major quay structures, the landing stage or the bridge pier-base recorded on the sites were erected before AD 60, but that all had been established before c AD 100.

Pottery

Pottery is the most common find on Roman sites and its analysis may help to suggest the status and function of associated buildings, or even to study the contemporary pattern of distribution and industrial organisation (see Chapter 10). However, a more common use is as a dating medium, since certain types are known to have been manufactured at specific times (Fig. 23; Pl. 2b). Consequently,

whenever these types are found in association with features recorded on an excavation, a date range for the activity represented by the features can be suggested. For example, a pit containing pottery from a kiln which was in production from AD 200 –250 cannot have been infilled before AD 200, although backfilling may have taken place substantially later than AD 250. However, if the pit also contained a large group of pottery in which no types known to have been introduced by AD 200– 250 were found, it could be argued that it may have been infilled before the mid-third century.

Pottery dating is based on the stratigraphic associations of certain types of pottery, some of which are more 'datable' than others. Dating parameters are constantly being refined as kiln sites are researched and published and new evidence is collated from securely-dated archaeological contexts. The discovery of coins often helps to date the associated pottery but it must be remembered that the coins may have been in circulation for some time before deposition. A further compli-

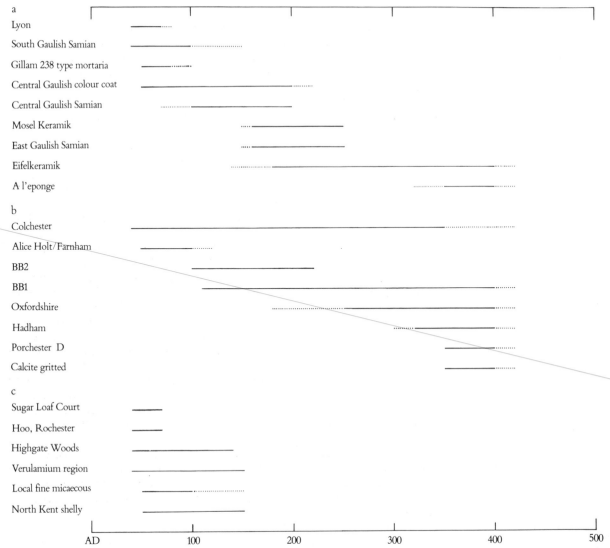

a
Lyon
South Gaulish Samian
Gillam 238 type mortaria
Central Gaulish colour coat
Central Gaulish Samian
Mosel Keramik
East Gaulish Samian
Eifelkeramik
A l'eponge

b
Colchester
Alice Holt/Farnham
BB2
BB1
Oxfordshire
Hadham
Porchester D
Calcite gritted

c
Sugar Loaf Court
Hoo, Rochester
Highgate Woods
Verulamium region
Local fine micaecous
North Kent shelly

| AD | 100 | 200 | 300 | 400 | 500 |

23 *The approximate date range for production of some of the kilns which supplied pottery for Roman London:* **a** *Continental,* **b** *British,* **c** *local. Once the sources of pottery types in an assemblage have been identified, then the group as a whole can be dated.*

cation is that pottery is also often redeposited and could therefore be considered residual in some contexts. In addition, certain types of pottery such as finewares and amphoras were often in use for longer than cooking pots. Amphoras in particular may have been reused as containers for other products and thus remained in use for as much as a century after their manufacture. However, it is generally possible to identify such earlier types in pottery groups, and to date the assemblage by its latest sherds, which are often in the freshest condition. Nevertheless, fragments of pottery are notoriously indestructible and many pits of Saxon date contain only Roman pottery initially discarded up to a thousand years earlier.

To help date the developments considered in this project, pottery from the recent waterfront sites was examined and identified, and the material from the Pudding Lane excavations (which was the largest site with the best structural sequence) was also quantified. All the information was sorted and grouped according to the stratigraphic site phasing supplied by the excavators. The most notable characteristic of the assemblage from Pudding Lane was that 77 per cent of the sherds quantified by weight were from amphoras, which, when measured against a mean value of 35 per cent from other contemporary sites elsewhere in London, suggests that this part of the waterfront was involved in commercial or mercantile activity. Similar high percentages of amphoras were recorded from the neighbouring Peninsular House excavations, but not at the Miles Lane site which was to the west of the Roman bridge. The proportion of samian found at Pudding Lane was also high, averaging 22 per cent by weight of the non-amphora assemblage. The samian was used and fairly abraded, and so was not thought to represent waterfront activity such as the unloading of cargoes or storage in a quayside warehouse. This contrasts with the mid-third-century assemblage from the St Magnus House site to the south (Richardson forthcoming). There were very few examples of even partially complete vessels or of joining sherds, and it is therefore possible that most of the pottery from the waterfront sites near Pudding Lane represent redeposited domestic refuse. This suggestion is supported by the character of the assemblage which has a similar percentage of imported pottery to that found on contemporary domestic sites, once the high proportion of amphoras is discounted.

The pottery most useful for dating purposes was the samian ware. Most of the thirty-eight stamped samian bases from Pudding Lane came from the quay infills and foreshores, and could be dated between AD 40 and 100, with most from the period AD 50–80 (Pl. 2a). The unstamped samian seemed to be broadly contemporary. It was noticeable that there seemed to be little difference in the types of pottery found in the deposits associated with both the landing stage and the first infilled east quay. Not only did the stamps fall into the same date range, but the work of the same potter, Passienus from La Graufesenque in South Gaul, occurred in both phases. However, many of the non-samian pottery types in these deposits were of the types usually dated to AD 55–65. This suggests that the pottery was redeposited from elsewhere, or had been in use for twenty or so years before it was discarded. Although the infill of the next quay also contained samian of the same date range as the preceding one, the coarsewares and non-samian finewares were later types. This quay may therefore be contemporary with the extension at Miles Lane which also contained early second-century pottery.

Datable pottery was also recovered from features associated with later activity on the waterfront. Large quantities of mid- and late second-century pottery came from deposits related to phases of drain construction, infilling, levelling and dumping from the Miles Lane site, and again, the composition of this pottery did not appear to reflect specifically waterfront or commercial activity. The material from the fire debris at the Pudding Lane sites was also of mid-late second-century date, and contained Central Gaulish black colour-coated ware which should be no earlier than cAD 160, and samian ware forms (Dr 40 and Dr 45) which should be no earlier than cAD 170. This suggests that the area was levelled for rebuilding in cAD 160–180. A substantial early third-century group examined from a drain fill on the Pudding Lane site contained pottery comparable with the large group from the infill of the early third-century quay at St Magnus House to the south (Richardson, forthcoming). This supports the suggestion that the third-century quay and drain found on different sites were constructed at around the same time (Chapter 2, Fig. 17b). The latest Roman layers on the Pudding Lane sites produced pottery of fourth-century date, which is rare in London. This material included the types known as Porchester D, Oxford red, á l'éponge and B wares.

Pottery study was therefore of considerable importance to the dating framework, especially for the phases from which neither coins nor dendrochronological samples were obtained.

Coins

Since most official Roman coins carry the head of an emperor or empress and a legend, it is normally possible to deduce the year (and sometimes even the place) in which a given example was minted (Pl. 3). Thus, unlike almost every other object found on archaeological sites, coins are *intrinsically* datable: it is not necessary to establish typologies, to examine their material composition or to analyse the relationships between many overlapping assemblages in order to find out when they were made. The two main drawbacks to the use of coins for dating are that they are much rarer finds than potsherds, and that they could remain in circulation for a considerable period of time before being lost. However, as will be shown below, there were also periods of rapid inflation when the Roman government demonetarised earlier issues rendering them valueless, so that coins remained in circulation for only a very short time.

A total of 97 Roman coins was recovered from the excavations west of Pudding Lane, 15 from those to the east, and nine from the Miles Lane sites. In view of their potential importance as dating evidence, cleaning and identifying them was regarded as a major priority. Most of the coins from Pudding Lane in particular were in poor condition, having thick corrosion layers that obscured or obliterated detail. All were X-radiographed before cleaning. The X-ray image gave an indication of the detail preserved and also now serves as an archival record of the coin. Examination and mechanical cleaning were carried out under a stereomicroscope, essential for detecting detail or traces of evidence such as silver plating within the corrosion layers. Because of the hardness of the corrosion, many of the Pudding Lane coins required chemical as well as mechanical cleaning. This was followed by thorough washing in baths of deionized water. The coins were stabilized and protected by soaking in a corrosion inhibitor and finally by coating with a lacquer developed for copper alloys.

Despite this careful treatment, many of the coins were still too badly damaged for identification. However, 59 could be identified precisely and a further 21 were assigned to a particular century. In general, therefore, the coins were either too few or too badly preserved to refine the chronological framework already established by dendrochronology and pottery for the erection of the quays and warehouses, although they lent support to it (Figs. 18 and 19). Their main contribution was to enable the later Roman phases to be dated. For example, it was possible to show that the infilling of the main drain to the east of the bridge and the final modifications to Building 6 did not take place before the second half of the fourth century. The pottery of this period is less susceptible to close dating and none of these late Roman features was associated with timber structures from which dendrochronological samples could be taken.

When the main excavations south of Thames Street are also taken into consideration, a total of 162 identifiable coins is produced. The pattern of coin loss seems to represent relatively continuous activity from the first to the end of the fourth century, with over 100 third- and fourth-century coins providing a strong argument for occupation on the waterfront throughout the late Roman period. This contrasts markedly with the pattern from recent excavation sites to the west of the Walbrook Stream away from the harbour. However, both areas have produced a large number of irregular late third-century issues.

Of additional interest was the discovery of three coin hoards. Two of these, comprising six and seven coins respectively, clearly belonged to the fourth century, but unfortunately the details were quite illegible. They were found in deposits associated with Building 6 (Chapter 11), just to the west of Pudding Lane. The third hoard was recovered from a silt layer overlying the remains of the fish-processing building (Chapter 8), and consisted of seven coins (Fig. 24). Several of them were corroded together, but unfortunately no trace of the container – perhaps a leather purse or bag – was found.

The hoard presumably represents the savings of person who lived in the area in the 280s, but why does it contain these particular coins and why were they lost? The answers perhaps lie in the complicated politics of the third century. In 259 the general Postumus was proclaimed emperor of Gaul, Spain and Britain, and for nearly fifteen years these provinces were managed by a series of 'rebel' emperors separately from the 'official' Roman administration. Two of the coins in the hoard, those of the Tetrici, are issues of this 'Gallic Empire'. Such coins are common finds on British sites and were so debased (containing less than 1 per cent silver) as to be almost worthless. In 273, however, the emperor Aurelian reunited the empire. Among his many administrative reforms, he undertook a major review of the coinage and *antoninani* were struck to a new standard. They are noticeably heavier, and metallurgical analysis has shown that they contain about 5 per cent silver. Numismatists believe that they were tariffed at a rate of one to five, or even one to ten, coins of the Gallic Empire. Four of the issues in the hoard, those of Aurelian's immediate successors Tacitus and Probus and of Magna Urbica, belong to just this series. In Britain they are much less widespread than pre-reform coinage, and it is likely that the hoarder deliberately selected them for their rarity and value.

However, in 286–7 Carausius was appointed commander of the fleet, but was soon proclaimed rebel emperor of Britain. Within a few years he issued his own series of coin, which circulated freely in the province. The owner of 'official'

Denomination	Emperor	Date	Mint	Ric
antoninianus	Quintillus	270	Rome	28
antoninianus	Tetricus I	270–73		
antoninianus	Tetricus II	270–73		
antoninianus	Tacitus	275–6	Ticinum	145
antoninianus	Tacitus	275–6	Gaul	65
antoninianus	Probus	276–82	Ticinum	516
antoninianus	Magna Urbica	284–5	Ticinum	347

24 *Coins from a third-century hoard found near Pudding Lane.*

coinage would now find that his treasure was out of favour or even worthless – he might discard it entirely or perhaps would store it away in the hope that its value would be restored. In the event, it was almost 1700 years before the hoard was rediscovered and its significance disclosed.

Conclusions

The three different methodologies therefore all contributed to the dating of the framework sug- gested by stratigraphic analysis. Dendro- chronology was especially important for the early part of the sequence, the coin study anchored the later phases in particular, while the pottery analysis supported that evidence and facilitated the dating of the intervening phases. Relative matching of part of the separate sequences from sites in the east, west and south of the study area was also achieved, primarily through the dendrochronological work and the study of pottery assemblages.

CHAPTER 4
BRIDGING THE THAMES

The search for the Roman bridge

If Roman London owed its prosperity to the Thames, it owed its position to the bridge, the physical requirements of which would have determined the choice of site. Certainly the first bridge must have been important, both as a stimulus and as a constraint, in the topographical development of the town. Although the existence of a bridge joining Roman London on the north bank of the Thames to the settlement on the Southwark shore is accepted, its nature and precise position has been the subject of considerable debate for over a century. That a Roman bridge did cross the river on a similar line to that of the medieval bridge at the foot of Fish Street Hill (Fig. 9) had long been suspected on the strength of the remarkable concentration of Roman finds in that location. The discovery was made during the demolition of the 650-year-old structure and the dredging of the river preparatory to the construction of John Rennie's bridge in 1824–31, and owes much to Charles Roach Smith, a noted antiquarian who made major contributions to the study of Roman London (Roach Smith 1859, 21–2). In addition, the main central entrance to the Forum lay at the head of a north-south street on the Gracechurch Street/Fish Street Hill alignment. The western side of such a street would correspond in the south with the gravel metalling against the eastern wall of a substantial first-century building observed fifty years ago on the Regis House site (Fig. 9; Marsh 1981, fig. 11.17).

By 1974, fresh evidence of converging road alignments on the south bank enabled Harvey Sheldon to argue 'with some degree of confidence' that the southern bridgehead 'was built on the site late occupied by its medieval successor, or very marginally upstream of it' (Merrifield and Sheldon 1974, 185). The northern abutment of the medieval bridge lay at the foot of Fish Street Hill, next to the church of St Magnus the Martyr, but intensive work by archaeologists in 1973–80, on sites to the

25 *Evidence from recent excavations suggests that the Romans built a timber bridge across the Thames, and a possible reconstruction is shown here.*

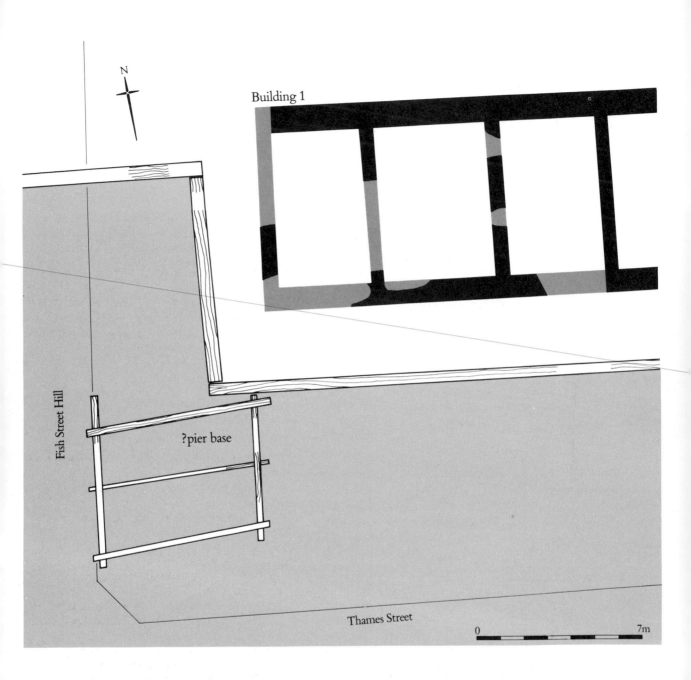

Building 1

N

Fish Street Hill

?pier base

Thames Street

0   7m

26 *A pier base for Roman London bridge?*
Excavations just east of Fish Street Hill in 1981
exposed this timber structure built out into the open
river to the south of the first-century quay.

east and west of it, failed to locate a major road or
any other feature which could suggest the precise
position of the Roman bridge. This important
negative evidence argues eloquently in favour of an
early bridge directly below Fish Street Hill itself.

A bridge discovered?

In the latter half of 1981, the excavation of the site
at the junction of Fish Street Hill and Lower
Thames Street exposed part of the late first-
century timber quay, which significantly turned
northwards at that point (Figs. 26–29; Pl. 4a).
Substantial traces of a braced timber box-structure
some 7m east-west were also examined, built out in
what had once been the open river on the foreshore,

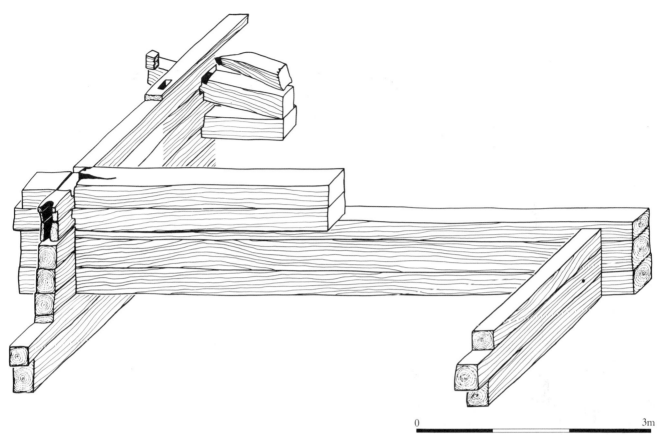

0 ▬▬▬▬▬▬▬ 3m

27 *Projection of the north face of the possible bridge pier base as recorded on site near Fish Street Hill.*

and extending across the line of the inlet. Unfortunately, the feature had been badly disturbed by nineteenth-century concrete foundations, but parts of its north and east walls were recorded during the controlled excavation and the bottom of the north-west corner was observed, albeit briefly, during the subsequent development of the site.

The east wall was traced for up to 3.5m north-south, but extended beyond the southern limit of excavation. It comprised eight timbers, the uppermost member of which was much decayed. They were horizontally-laid edge to edge and were on average 320mm by 250mm although the lowest two members were larger. There was evidence for three timbers lap-jointed through the east wall, serving as intermediate braces. The structure survived to a height of 2.2m, but the uppermost member had traces of a mortise cut into its upper face which penetrated the member beneath, suggesting that a

superstructure was once carried still higher. Parts of the north-east and north-west corners and a substantial section of the north wall were also recorded. The five squared timbers of the north wall were laid horizontally one on top of the other, and each was *c*320mm square in section. They had slots cut in their upper and lower faces at each end, to form the lap-joints which articulated with the east or west wall members.

A rectangular structure built of squared oak timbers, well-jointed at the corners and laterally braced, was therefore erected on the foreshore in the open river with its basal members set in a trench cut into the clay foreshore. It was *c*7m east-west by *c*5m north-south, assuming that the internal braces marked the middle of the feature. It must have been in position by the late first century, when the erection of the infilled eastern quay necessitated cutting away part of its north-eastern corner (Fig. 29), but after *c*AD 78, as the dendrochronological analysis shows (see Figs. 18, 21). Its superstructure must have been at least partially dismantled in the early second century, when the feature was infilled and engulfed by the deposits dumped to the south

and west of the late first-century quay during that phase of waterfront reclamation (Fig. 14d). The small section of the eastern wall which was excavated by Museum staff had been sealed by surfaces and then by a major destruction horizon of mid- to late second-century date.

What function could this enigmatic feature have served? It cannot represent a jetty or extension to the quay structures, since it was not joined to them and was on a different alignment, its northern wall following the Om contour. It sat at the mouth of an artificial inlet, the only indentation in the otherwise unbroken frontage recorded for 70m to east and to west, just south of a modest spur which projected slightly into the river (Fig. 11). This foreshore structure could clearly have supported a considerable load, and lay precisely in the area where a bridge foundation could reasonably be assumed to be. It was therefore suggested that it may represent one of a series of pier-bases which could have supported the carriageway of an early Roman timber bridge (Milne 1982).

The use of timber, rather than stone, need not preclude the interpretation of the feature as a bridge-pier, since the construction of the quays implies that this medium was readily available in quantity and that the necessary skills to exploit it were not lacking (Chapter 5). Similar-sized timbers were used in the bridge abutment at Aldwincle, Northants (Jackson and Ambrose 1976) as well as for bridge-piers themselves at Laupen and Mainz (Cuppers 1969, 185; 198). The last example is the closest parallel in its design (though not in respect of joinery used) to the London feature, but was twice the size, while the piers for the mid-first-century bridge over the Rhine at Koblenz were c7m by 4m (Fehr 1981, 287–301, fig. 2; Schieferdecker, 1981, 313–25, fig. 2). The piers shown on Fig. 32 have triangular-shaped (and aptly-named) cutwaters at one end. These are important features of bridge piers, since they help to protect the bridge substructure from the full force of the river by diverting the water around the sides of the foundations. Bridges on a tidal river might have cutwaters on both the upstream and downstream ends of their pier-bases. Had such features been unambiguously recorded with the London feature under discussion, then its identification as a bridge pier would have been more certain. Although at least five piles were observed close to its eastern face, it was just not possible to mount detailed excavations on the crucial areas to the east and west of it and so that particular question is unresolved.

There is nevertheless considerable evidence to support the existence of a Roman bridge at the foot of Fish Street Hill, not least because the first-century quay returned at that point, while the suggestion that the timber structure on the contemporary foreshore could represent part of such a bridge is not inconsistent with an assessment of its form and location.

Reconstructing the bridge

Given that Roman London was served by a bridge incorporating the feature discovered near Fish Street Hill, it is of considerable interest to know what it might have looked like. Firstly, it would have been built entirely of timber. That a wooden bridge would have been strong enough to span the Thames cannot be questioned: Caversham, Henley, Marlow, Maidenhead, Windsor, Staines, Chertsey and Kingston were all served by timber bridges in the medieval period (Rigold 1975, 50), while Datchet, Walton, Putney, Hampton, Kew and Battersea had major timber bridges built there as late as the eighteenth century, some of which survived into the age of photography (Croad 1983).

Roman bridges were supported by *piles* or *piers* (Fig. 30). The latter were usually masonry and could only be constructed across valleys in which the river ran dry in the summer months, unless coffer-dams were used or the water was temporarily diverted. The associated roadway was carried on arches which sprang from pier to pier but this superstructure could be either masonry, like the Pons Fabricus in Rome and the Ponte di Augusto at Rimini, or timber, like Apollodorus' bridge over the Danube depicted on Trajan's Column (Shirley Smith 1953, 11–23).

Pile bridges, on the other hand, were common on rivers whose beds were not exposed either by summer drought or tidal action. The most famous example is the bridge Julius Caesar claims to have thrown across the Rhine in only ten days, which

28 *The south west corner of the late first-century quay recorded near Fish Street Hill, surviving to its full height, looking east. A 1m scale rests on the working surface, with infill material removed to east and west revealing braces and earlier piles. In the foreground is the north wall of the possible bridge pier base, the rest of which is covered by modern concrete.*

a

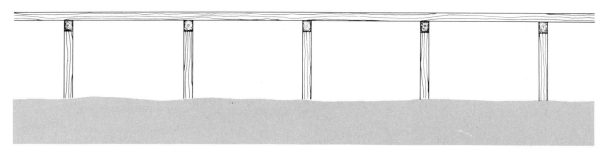

b

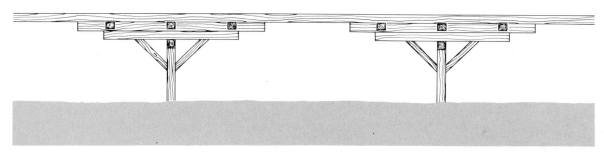

c

30 *Roman bridges could be supported by*
a *piles,* **b** *simple cantilever systems, or*
c *arches.*

29 *The possible bridge pier base with 0.5m scale*
must have been erected before the quay, since its
timbers were clearly cut to accommodate the front
wall of the quay in cAD *90.*

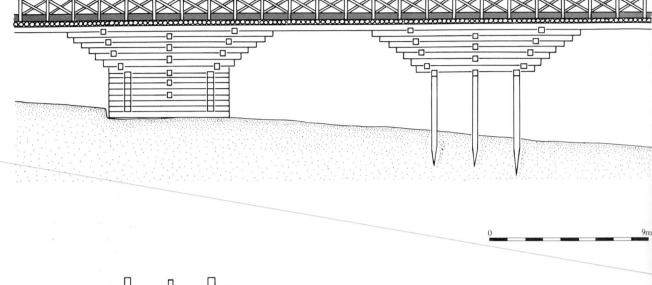

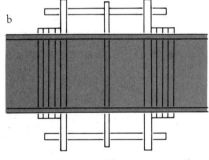

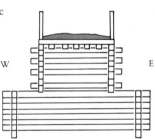

31 *Elevation of a possible reconstruction for Roman London bridge. The decking could be supported by timber pier bases in the shallow water and piled trestles in midstream.* **a** *western elevation* **b** *plan of pier base below road level* **c** *south facing elevation. Carriageway shown toned.*

was based on a series of trestles formed by driving piles into the river bed. The London feature is therefore unusual, though not unparalleled, in that it implies a timber bridge with wooden piers. This is consistent with the suggestion that the contemporary Thames was tidal, for the structure must have been erected at low tide on the exposed foreshore. Further out in the deep-water channel, the roadway must have been supported by piled trestles, as it would not have been possible to replicate the pier construction under water. The

Roman London bridge could therefore have incorporated both piers and piles.

Such a change in construction technique in midstream is also associated with the bridging of the River Mosel at Trier in Germany in the second century (Cuppers 1969). The publication of this project – which is a classic of its type – shows that a series of rectangular coffer-dams, each 27m by 14m, were constructed across the river. Once the water had been expelled from these substantial boxes, the foundations for the massive masonry piers were prepared and laid. The coffer-dams comprised an inner and outer wall of timber, with the intervening area packed with clay, rendering it water-tight. The walls around Piers I, V, VI and VII were constructed of squared baulks of timber lap-jointed at the corners: the style was so similar to the London pier that it was once thought that it too may have been a remnant of a coffer-dam, but its position and the lack of clay packing argue against this interpretation. In the middle of the River Mosel, however, where the bed was deeper, the coffer construction technique changed from horizontally-laid baulks to vertically-driven piles around Piers II–IV.

Since part of the London bridge may have been raised on piles, the decking itself is not likely to have been supported by arches, which are a feature of pier-based bridges (Fig. 30). It is, however, possible that a type of cantilever system may have been employed in which the span between two piers is supported by horizontally-laid timbers stacked one upon the other, but with the ends jutting out and overlapping each other in a stepped formation (Figs. 25, 31). This solution is the one which, it is argued, most readily fits the London evidence, requiring precisely the same expertise and size of timbers as were already used in the foundation, so that all the necessary technology was unquestionably to hand. According to H. Shirley-Smith, timber cantilever bridges can still be found in the East. The bridge over the River Jhelum at Srinagar, the capital of Kashmir, was built with piers of horizontal logs laid in courses alternately east-west and north-south with the logs

in each successive row being longer than the one beneath. A similar system has also been recorded in Norway (Shirley-Smith 1953, 6–7, fig. 2). A less complex form of cantilever support which operates with piled trestles is shown on Fig. 30 and is based on the Reichenbach bridge, Munich (A. Butcher, pers comm). Thus a roadway supported on a simple cantilever system with foundations of both piers and piles could be a practical proposition.

If the width between the piers was at least 6–7m and if the roadway was at $c + 5$m OD, then there would be sufficient clearance for a ship of a similar size to the Blackfriars I type to pass through at low tide with its mast lowered (see Chapter 9). The carriageway itself could have been formed with hurdles or a corduroy bed of logs over which clay and gravel was packed, a technique not dissimilar to that used for the Roman roads which crossed marshy ground on their approach to the southern end on the bridge (Bird *et al* 1978, 59–61). Since the pier itself was probably only *c*7m wide east-west, the roadway may only have been 4–5m wide,

32 *Roman timber bridge piers:* **a** *Mainz, plan and elevation* **b** *Laupen, plan* **c** *London, plan.*

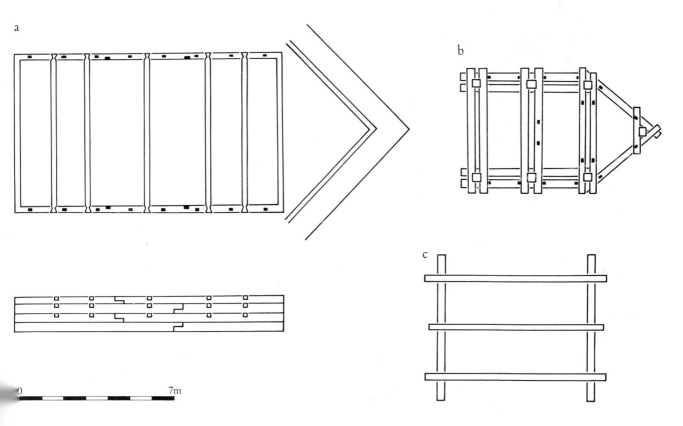

which is considerably narrower than the minimum width of 6–8m recorded for the roads which led to it (Bird *et al* 1978, 22–7). The bridge crossed the Thames at the narrowest point, taking advantage of the slight spur on the north bank and, more significantly, the large island on the southern side (Fig. 49b, c). It is even possible that there may have been other islands in mid-stream which the Roman engineers could have incorporated in the actual course of the bridge itself.

Three Roman London bridges?

Other problems also need to be solved before the exact alignment of the bridge can be established, the most important of which concerns the late first-century dating of the timber pier-base (Figs. 18, 21). Since the roads converging on the southern bridgehead are thought to be of mid–first-century date, the existence of a bridge constructed some thirty years earlier than the structure associated with the pier-base is implied. That feature could therefore be London's first bridge and the structure described in this chapter its replacement. Since the pier-base was engulfed in the reclamation deposits associated with an early second-century advance of the waterfront, it is even possible to argue that the bridge may have been rebuilt again at this time. The replacement bridges, however many there may have been, would probably not have been erected directly over the line of the predecessor, but just to one side of it. Such was certainly the case at Trier when a timber bridge was replaced by a masonry structure in AD 140, as well as in nineteenth-century London, where the medieval bridge remained in use until Rennie's bridge was opened in 1831 just 25m upstream.

That Roman London was served by a bridge seems certain and evidence from excavations on both banks strongly suggests that the most likely line was close to that of the medieval bridge. Detailed support for the suggestion that the timber feature found near Fish Street Hill was part of the substructure of a bridge has been presented. However, even this identification cannot be proved conclusively, so it follows that the reconstruction considered in this chapter must be treated with caution. Although some old questions have been answered, new questions have been raised. Controversy over the bridge will therefore continue simply because its history is such a vital element in the development of both the town and the province: in the Roman period at least seven major routes began or ended at London and the bridge was the very centre of that crucial network (Fig. 84).

CHAPTER 5

ROMAN QUAY CONSTRUCTION

In 1961 a seminal essay on Roman timber building techniques began: 'Actual remains of Roman timber buildings are rare: timber does not survive for long, except under conditions so unusual as to be ruled out of normal experience' (Richmond 1961, 15). Almost 25 years later, sufficient examples of well-preserved ancient wooden structures have been recorded to show that the conditions necessary for their survival are encountered far more often than was previously supposed. Provided timber is buried within an environment from which oxygen (and therefore the destructive action of bacteria) is excluded, then it will survive for thousands of years, as the discovery of the mesolithic brushwood platform at Star Carr and the neolithic trackways and hurdles in Somerset shows (Clarke 1954; Coles 1975–83).

In addition to the possible bridge pier described in Chapter 4, three more massive timber waterfront structures of first-century date were recorded in London, preserved in the waterlogged deposits. They survived to heights of over 2.5m in places, and were traced for lengths of up to 70m. Their detailed study is important for three main reasons. Firstly, an assessment of these spectacular structures as structures provides insights into Roman civil engineering practices. Secondly, study of the timbers as examples of worked wood reveals details of Roman joinery and timberworking (cf Weeks 1982) to complement the evidence gained by examination of buildings (Maloney 1982), boats (Marsden 1967) and wells (Wilmott 1982). Thirdly, analysis of the wood itself can reveal details about the contemporary trees, woods, and woodland management, as well as providing material for general dendrochronological study (Chapter 3).

Each of the three waterfront structures considered in this chapter shared common attributes, but represent three somewhat different solutions to the same problem, that of erecting substantial works actually in the open river. But before a general assessment is attempted, the structure and form of each feature will be described in turn.

The western quay, cAD 70

Traces of a feature thought to be a first-century quay were found to the west of London Bridge in the 1920s (Lambert 1921) and fifty years later Louise Miller supervised the controlled excavation of an additional section of the structure, while the subsequent watching brief on the 3000sq.m site finally established the form and alignment of a 62m length of the quay (Miller 1982). It had been built in sections from east to west, and although these sections differed in detail, they shared common characteristics (Figs. 34, 40c).

Trenches were dug in the foreshore to allow the base of the front wall to be laid more or less level at cOrdnance Datum. The massive beams were laid end to end, joined by scarf joints. Twelve members were recorded in the lowest tier, with lengths varying from 2.5 to 8.5m, and cross-sections from 450×460mm to 480×730mm. In the first phase of construction there were four or five other horizontal beams in the front wall, bringing the top of the quay to $c + 2$m OD, although this was subsequently raised to $c + 3$m with the addition of more beams. Again, there was no standard size for these timbers, which were of smaller cross-section than the basal members, varying from 200×400mm to 400×460mm. Scarf joints were used to join the ends of some of these timbers. Other members were only held in position by their own weight and by the braces which tied the south wall to the less substantial north wall and to the natural river bank. The braces articulated with the south wall by means of lap joints, and their heads protruded southwards into the Roman river by up to 0.5m.

Twenty-two sets of braces were recorded on the site, incorporating members from 3.65 to 5.9m long and of similar cross-section to the upper members of the south wall. The number of braces in each set varied from two to seven, and the spacing was also irregular (Fig. 34). For example, those which were south of the east walls of Buildings B and D (Fig. 14b) were only 1m apart, while others were up to 4m apart. The alignment of

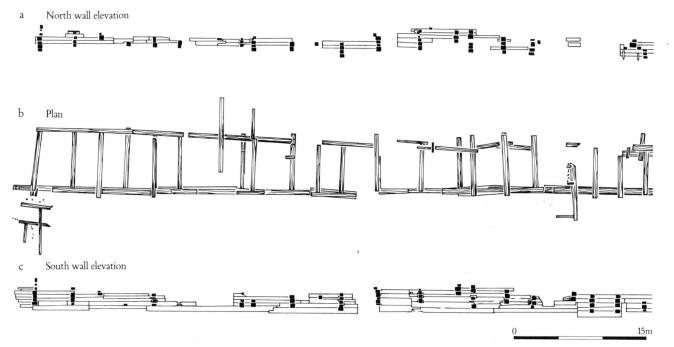

a North wall elevation

b Plan

c South wall elevation

0   15m

34 *Plan and elevations of the* AD 70 *quay timbers recorded near Miles Lane, west of London bridge (see Fig. 14).* **a** *north wall elevation* **b** *plan* **c** *south wall elevation.*

the north wall differed from that of the south wall, the distance between them varying from 3m to 5.35m. There were at most only three beams in the north wall, up to 380 × 520mm in cross-section.

In the west of the site, a small jetty projected at least 5m southwards from the south wall, perhaps marking an access point at the southern end of a street or alley. To the east was another projection, this time built as an integral part of the quay to accommodate the main timber-lined drain west of Building A (Fig. 34).

In several places, evidence for two phases of construction of quay and buildings was recorded. The main body of the quay was infilled and initially surfaced with flint, ragstone and tile rubble. The second phase saw the ground surface raised by up to 1m, and may have incorporated a planked floor over part of the quay.

The landing stage, cAD 80

The remains of a timber landing stage were recorded in the controlled excavations to the west of Pudding Lane (Fig. 14b). It was laid out parallel to the gravel bank and revetments which formed

33 *The south-west corner of the Roman quay near Fish Street Hill, looking south. Although 2000 years old, the massive timbers of the first-century quay survived in excellent condition.*

the early phase of waterfront modification (Chapter 2, Fig. 14a), but on a slightly different alignment to that of the conjectured bridge pier and of the natural contours. Although it had been extensively robbed in antiquity, enough survived to show that horizontally-laid, squared timbers stacked one upon the other formed the solid west and south walls as well as the regularly spaced braces. The north wall was a more open build, incorporating massive vertical members at c2m intervals rising from a base-plate (Fig. 35a). Each vertical member was tied to the south wall by braces lapped to its east face (Fig. 36). An open timber framework presumably supporting a planked platform and built out into the open river is indicated. This is interpreted as a landing stage, designed to facilitate the passage of men or merchandise from ship to shore.

Two courses of the west wall survived, comprising timbers at least 3.7m long, and c300 by 300mm in cross-section. Both tiers incorporated two horizontally-laid timbers butted edge-to-edge, articulating with the three surviving members of the south wall by means of lap joints (Fig. 40a).

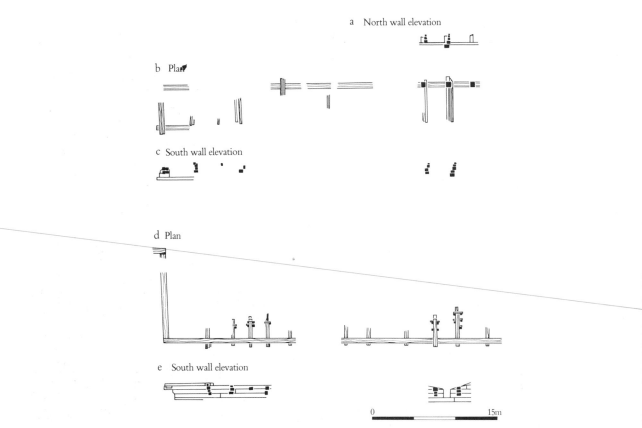

a North wall elevation

b Plan

c South wall elevation

d Plan

e South wall elevation

0   15m

35 *Plans and elevations of the landing stage and later first-century quay timbers recorded near Pudding Lane, east of London bridge. Landing stage:* **a** *north wall elevation* **b** *plan* **c** *south wall elevation;*
AD *90 quay:* **d** *plan* **e** *south wall elevation.*

The back of the structure was only examined in detail in the centre of the excavations, where a substantial length of the base-plate was traced (Fig. 35a). Three substantial vertical members were recorded on that base-plate, and evidence for two more on the same alignment was observed to east and west. These members had all been truncated at a height of $c + 1.5$m OD, but had been held in position by sets of three squared braces (Fig. 36). The lowest brace not only articulated with the base-plate but was also nailed to the vertical post, effectively stabilising the base of the structure. The vertical post itself simply sat directly on the base-plate. Significantly, a mortise-and-tenon joint was not used, although that would have been the solution adopted by a medieval carpenter in an analogous situation. The south end of the braces

had been severed at the point where they would have joined the south wall, and the steep south-north slope of the cut line presumably reflects the angle at which the front wall was listing when it was dismantled.

The regular line of squared piles driven against both edges of the northern base-plate seems to have been an integral part of the landing stage, but the function of six pile groups at the west end of the structure is less easy to explain (Fig. 28). A number of interpretations are possible: they may represent the base of a stair onto the bridge which lay immediately to the west, or the remains of a temporary structure erected after the landing stage collapsed but before the later quay was infilled, for example. Just to the north of the projected line of the front wall of the structure was a further series of squared piles. They were over 2m long, and had

36 *Part of the braced north wall of the openwork landing stage built out over the pottery-strewn foreshore (0.5m scale), looking north. Recorded near Pudding Lane beneath quay shown in Fig. 38.*

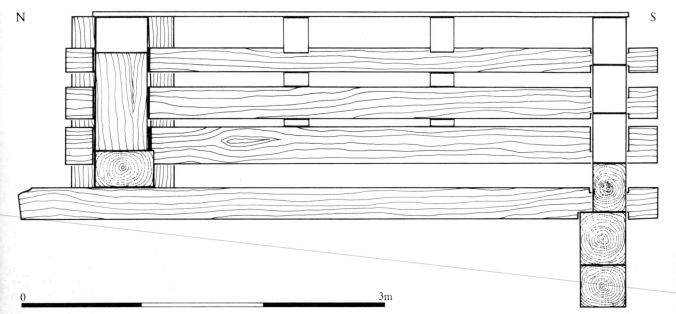

N   S

0   3m

37 *Composite side elevation of first-century*
landing stage partially reconstructed. Timbers with
grain recorded on site.

been driven in pairs at 1–2m centres. The exact
purpose which they served is uncertain, but it
seems likely that they supported the front wall in
some way. Most seemed to be sealed by the infill
dumps of the later quay with which they cannot
therefore have functioned.

The eight sets of braces recorded during the
controlled excavation and the subsequent moni-
toring of the site in 1981–2 were regularly spaced
and there seems little doubt that they all represent
parts of the same structure. The line of the north,
south and west walls of the landing stage was
therefore established, but its eastern extent is
uncertain. However, some of the braces observed
during the watching brief to the east of the area in
1980 must be associated with this structure rather
than with the later quay (described below) which
was superimposed upon it. The landing stage
therefore extended at least 35m east-west, and
possibly as much as 57m. The framework was not
infilled, but was left open, since sandy waterlaid
deposits built up within it, while in the west a huge
dump of oyster shells accumulated both inside and
outside the structure (Chapter 8).

Part of a suggested reconstruction of this structure is shown on Fig. 37. The timber decking
would have been laid on the uppermost member of
the south wall, joists being laid across the braces

and on a major east-west beam supported on the
vertical posts rising from the north wall base-plate.
Since there was no evidence of a carpentered joint
such as a tenon cut on the head of the surviving
posts, it is possible that the beam was only held in
place by the heads of the squared piles driven into
the foreshore against the edges of the northern
base-plate. However, a system similar to that used
to join the foot of the vertical member to the base-
plate may have been utilised. It is not certain
exactly at what height the decking would have
functioned, but it must have been at or above
$c + 1.9$m OD, the level of the highest surviving head
of the piles set against the northern base-plate.

The eastern quay, cAD 90

A subsequent development of this eastern section
of the waterfront involved the establishment of an
infilled timber-faced quay, which provided a level
artificial terrace at the foot of the hillside (Fig. 14c;
Pls. 1, 4b). Evidence of the substantial timber
revetments which formed the facing of the quay
itself was recovered from sites both east and west of
Pudding Lane (Figs. 35d, e). Similarities in form,
alignment and date suggest that they were part of
the same structure, the total length of which would
have been at least 75m east-west. The erection of
two ranges of masonry buildings, Buildings 1 and 2
described in Chapter 6, was closely associated with
this construction phase.

Much of the landing stage was carefully dismantled, but the site was not completely cleared. The

elements which were retained included the lowest
two courses of the west wall and the braced vertical
members on the northern base-plate, as described
in the previous section. The timbers of the west
wall of the new quay were laid directly over the
remains of the landing stage, while the obsolete
vertical members were incorporated in the southern faces of the masonry foundations for Buildings
1 and 2 to provide additional stability at that point.
Since the position of the buildings closely follows
the form of the landing stage, in that the bay walls
are aligned and founded on the north end of each
alternate set of braces, it seems reasonable to

38 *Detail of the eastern quay, looking north-east,
showing the front face supported by braces (0.5m
scale). The infill deposits have been half-sectioned
revealing the braces of the earlier landing stage.
See Pl. 1.*

assume that the buildings had been designed
before the landing stage was demolished specifically to incorporate the vertical members. This
implies that the landing-stage did not simply
collapse and was immediately repaired, but was
dismantled and replaced as part of a deliberate plan

61

which integrated the construction of contemporary quays, terraces and buildings.

The unbraced timbers of the west wall were traced for at least 4m northwards and apparently extended as far as the 1.5m contour. The west wall incorporated two courses of massive timbers up to 660 × 400mm in cross section, laid one upon the other face to face, and superimposed directly upon the lowest two tiers of the landing stage. A much decayed timber was all that survived of the uppermost fifth tier.

The south wall comprised at least five courses of oak baulks horizontally laid face to face, stacked one upon the other. The roughly squared timbers were from 2.5 to 6.7m long and varied considerably in cross-section from 280 × 450mm to 460 × 630mm. The wall was founded on the remnants of the landing-stage in the west, on squared piles in the middle and on substantial horizontally-laid timber wedges in the east of the excavations. It was braced at irregular intervals of between 2–4m by stacks of two or three tie-backs aligned north-south. Twelve sets of braces were recorded on the sites to the west of Pudding Lane, and some of the fourteen observed to the east must also have been associated with this quay. The braces articulated with the upper courses of the south wall by means of lap joints (Fig. 40b). Their southern ends protruded into the Roman river and their northern ends were secured by pile-retained cross-pieces. Many of the braces were obviously reused timbers.

An aperture cut into the south wall accommodated a second-century drain when excavated (Pl. I), but that drain seems to have replaced a first-century feature which had occupied a similar position. The aperture itself is thought to be an integral part of the original construction of the quay face.

A mistake in the setting-out of the structure was recorded in the south-west corner. Here the line of the quay's south wall diverged sufficiently from that of the landing stage to necessitate cutting back the end of the east wall of the conjectured bridge pier (Fig. 29). This proves, incidentally, that the pier was unequivocally in position in the open river before the late first-century quay was erected. The unsightly use of wedges to complete the build of this corner (Fig. 39) demonstrates that construction must have terminated here, and therefore must have proceeded from east to west, as was also the case with the western quay of cAD 70.

The inside of the timber framework was infilled with a variety of dumped deposits which sealed the contemporary tie-backs as well as the truncated members of the earlier landing-stage. The quay was levelled off with a surface of brickearth and gravel at $c + 2$m OD.

Civil engineering and Roman joinery

Of these three first-century structures, the landing stage clearly contrasts with the other two in terms of the uniform size of timber used and in the careful, regular spacing of the braces. The little that did survive was sufficient to show that it was a relatively sophisticated structure and that its principal elements were presumably prefabricated, since it had to be erected on an open foreshore between tides.

The other two structures showed marked irregularities in form, most notably in the alignment of the north wall of the western quay, as well as in the sizes of timber used. The spacing and number of braces articulating with each tier also differed, features which reflect the varied lengths of the timbers forming the south wall, each one of which needed to be braced at least at its eastern and western ends. Had standard lengths of timber been used to form the front wall, then all the braces could have been at more regular intervals. The general implication is therefore that, although the timbers must have been brought to the site ready squared, the cutting of most of the joints necessary to erect the structure was done on site as work progressed and as timber became available, rather than by adhering rigidly to a blueprint. Nevertheless, all three structures would have required heavy lifting gear, ropes and piling rams as well as saws, axes and so forth (Liversidge 1976), although only in the setting out of the landing stage would anything other than the simplest surveying equipment have been used.

The chance survival of an unfinished joint on which the toolmarks had not been removed proved instructive (Fig. 41). It showed that the lap joint was marked out by sawing deep cuts at either end, after which the intervening wood was cleared out with axes. It also demonstrated that Roman engineers were capable of making mistakes, since the joint was clearly in the wrong place.

39 *Late first-century jerry building. Irregular wedges were used to complete the south-west corner of this quay, showing that construction must have ended here, having begun in the east. 0.5m scale.*

a
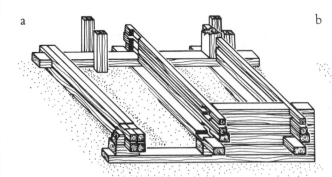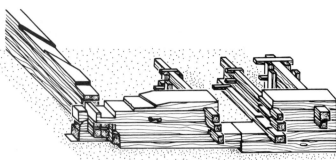

c
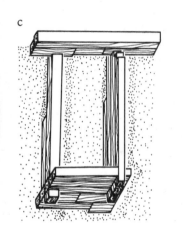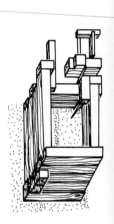

d
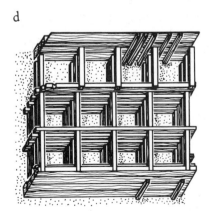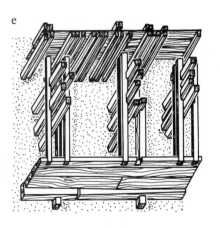

0   5m

Rather than reflecting a private merchant's individual enterprise, the scale of the harbour works clearly implies an official involvement. In an occupied territory such as Britain was in the first century, the army would presumably have designed and organised the project. Such schemes were very labour intensive, but whether the man power was provided by the military directly, or by civilian labourers or slaves under military supervision is a matter for speculation. Suffice it to say that the handling of massive timbers and the erection of the waterfront structures on a tidal foreshore would have required considerable organisation, even though two of the structures were neither elegantly designed nor expertly erected.

The Roman waterfront structures contrast noticeably with their medieval counterparts. Of some twenty examples of twelfth- to fifteenth-century riverfront revetments recorded in London, all were of much slighter construction, rarely incorporating individual timbers of the prodigious size found in the first-century structures. Nevertheless, the medieval revetments were as effective as the Roman but were more economical in their use of timber, often utilising wood from trees eighty years old or less when felled. The base of the G10 revetment erected in the mid-fourteenth century near Trig Lane was still operative almost a century later, for example (Milne and Milne 1982). In addition, the erection of the medieval revetments could have been accomplished by much smaller teams than would have been required to install the Roman structures.

Superficially, the limited range and poor quality of the Roman joinery exhibited in these constructions seems to say more about the conditions under which they were built than about the general standard of contemporary carpentry. Nevertheless, at least one observation of wider significance for the study of Roman joinery can be made, given that there must have been at least some connection between practices used on the waterfront and those found in contemporary buildings on dry land. All the braces in the three first-century structures considered in this chapter and in the pier-base described in Chapter 3 were *lap-jointed* to the wall members, with the result that the heads of the braces protruded beyond the main body of the structure. By contrast, the second- and third-century waterfront structures found at the Custom House and St Magnus House sites (Figs. 40d, e) used *dovetail joints* to effect this crucial join, which left a neat vertical face to those quays. Since there are few examples of Roman vernacular carpentry in Britain it is difficult to argue for a major change in techniques in the second century on the evidence of the waterfront installations alone. However, a recent survey of timber-lined wells provides an instructive parallel, for it shows that in the first and second century such structures utilised half-lap joints to form the corners, but by the late second to early third century more sophisticated dovetail and bridled joints became the standard response (Wilmott 1982, 26–30; figs. 19–21). In other words, a second-century change from the use of simple lap-joints to joints such as dovetails which require more careful marking out occurs in two quite distinct classes of timberwork, wells and waterfront structures. This change may therefore be symptomatic of a more general development.

Timber supply: British oaks and the cedars of Lebanon

The Romans are known to have imported timber supplies over large distances (Meiggs 1980), but there is no reason to suspect that the majority of the wood used for the London waterfront development was anything other than British, since it was all oak. Much of it was cut from tall, straight-grained 200–300-year-old trees of the type that would have grown in dense woodland. Nevertheless, there is no evidence of economy or care in the Roman use of timber. Baulks between 4–7m long were common, while some were almost 9m in length and most of the logs had simply been squared. In some instances, only one major structural timber had been cut from each tree, a wasteful practice which contrasts noticeably with later medieval techniques. For example, a study of the thirteenth-century roof of the Blackfriars Priory at Gloucester has shown that four rafters, two collars, four sole pieces and one scissor brace were cut from a single oak (Rackham et al 1978, fig. 7).

The wasteful use of timber on the Roman waterfront seems to imply that large areas within relatively easy reach of London were covered with dense woodland. Dr Hanson has calculated that to build a standard Roman fort of four acres internal

40 *Roman waterfront structures from London. First-century:* **a** *landing stage and* **b** *quay near Pudding Lane;* **c** *sections of the* AD *70 quay near Miles Lane. Second-century:* **d** *partial reconstruction of Custom House quay. Third-century:* **e** *partial reconstruction of quay from St Magnus House site.*

41 *Roman carpentry. Detail of an unfinished lap-joint with saw cuts marking the ends. Axes were clearly used to cut away the timber in the joint itself. 10 × 10mm scale.*

area, the volume of timber required for the associated buildings and defences would call for the clear felling of 16–30 acres of British woodland (Hanson 1978, 298). Given this and a profligate use of timber, the London waterfront structures suggest that many acres of hitherto dense woodland must have been cleared to facilitate the laying out of settlements, roads and fields and to provide the timber to build and roof whole new towns. The Roman impact on the landscape must have been considerable.

The choice of timber rather than stone for the third-century quay (Miller *et al*, forthcoming) is of especial interest. By that date, the logistical problems of transporting Kentish ragstone to London in quantity had been solved, as the construction of the landward defensive wall amply demonstrates (Maloney 1983). Indeed, the fact that much of the new building within the third-century town was also in masonry could suggest that timber was not so easily available as it had been previously. Therefore the use of timber for the contemporary harbour installations demonstrates not only an actual preference for that material, but also the substantial stands of ancient woodland had survived up to that date.

Documentary evidence of timber supplies and prices in the Roman Empire in the late third century suggest that lengths of oak up to 7m long were to be sold at no more than 6 *denarii* per square foot, by far the cheapest timber available at the time, presumably because it was the most common. By contrast, pine or fir of a type not found in Britain was up to thirteen times more expensive but could be obtained in very much longer lengths

(Meiggs 1982, 366–7). Nevertheless, fragments and objects of non indigenous wood have been found in waterlogged deposits from Roman London, as recent research by V. Straker has shown, but these items do not represent a trade in unworked exotic timber for the building industry. For example, most of the barrels from London sites are made from cedar or silver fir (see Chapter 10), and were imported as containers of continental wine rather than as boards to be made up into barrels in a British coopers yard. Most of the twenty-two fragments of writing tablets recovered from the recent waterfront excavations were of the wax-impressed type made from larch, cedar or silver fir, suggesting that they too were brought over as finished products. Only one box wood writing tablet could have been British-made and, significantly, was of the carbon-ink variety.

In conclusion, it can be said that the Romans had no need to import exotic timber to Britain, since there is ample evidence that the province was extensively wooded. Nevertheless, supplying sufficient building timber for a town like London could have caused considerable inroads into that resource unless some form of woodland management was practised. Certainly there are Roman records of the coppicing of chestnut cut every five to seven years and oak every seven to ten years to meet the fuel needs of local towns profitably (Meiggs 1982, 268–9). However, the lavish use of ancient timber on the London waterfront suggests that the Romans saw much of the British woodland as a resource to exploit rather than to develop. In doing so, they would have opened up large areas of previously impenetrable forest and thus the timber structures on the London waterfront represent not only the scale of urban expansion but also that of rural development.

WAREHOUSING IN ROMAN LONDON

Anyone visiting London's Dockland 50 years ago could not fail to be impressed by the many acres of vast warehouses, packed with goods from every part of the globe. The provision of temporary and long-term storage buildings was indeed a prerequisite for any 'trading' centre and the scale of this provision provides a useful index of the scope of a port's commercial activity. In this chapter, it is suggested that one way of understanding the Roman port and the scale and scope of the 'trade' – or rather traffic in goods – which passed through it, is to identify the areas of contemporary warehousing and to derive from an examination of the form of individual buildings some idea of their specific function. However, before the evidence for storage buildings in Roman London is discussed, the nature of such structures elsewhere in the Roman Empire will be reviewed.

Roman storage buildings have generally been discussed by archaeologists in three categories: military (Gentry 1976; Manning 1975b); rural, which usually refers to simple granaries on farms and villas (Morris 1979); and urban storage buildings, which form the most interesting point of comparison here. Professor Rickman has made authoritative surveys (Rickman 1971) of all three types and his observations on urban storage buildings are particularly relevant. As he points out, buildings for both long and short term storage of a variety of goods ranging from foodstuffs to building materials are known from many parts of the Empire, but their forms are as varied as their functions and the goods stored in them. The word used by the Romans to designate any kind of storage building was *horrea*, in the plural, rather than the singular *horreum* (Rickman 1971, 1). This was presumably because a *horrea* was thought of as a single building complex comprising a number of individual units, each one a *horreum*.

Horrea in Roman Britain and the Empire

The majority of storage buildings which have been excavated in Britain were military granaries. Char-

acteristics of these are pest and damp-proof floors (cement, flagstone or planking raised on piles), usually with provision for ventilation underneath the floor, and long narrow rooms with buttresses or strengthened walls to take the weight of the grain. No attempt has yet been made to assess urban warehousing in Britain and only a few Roman harbourside storage buildings have as yet been identified. The interpretation of a building at Chester as a warehouse is acknowledged to be tentative by the excavators (Strickland and Ward 1981, 106) and, although the existence of a quayside granary at York is more certain, its identification is almost entirely dependent on environmental evidence with insufficient structural detail to make possible significant comparisons with the London buildings (Kenward and Williams 1979). The two early timber structures near Fishbourne palace identified as storage buildings incorporated rows of pile-holes implying a raised timber floor, but no elements of the superstructure survived (Cunliffe 1971, 39–42).

In complete contrast there are the enormous complexes of storage buildings in Rome and its ports Ostia and Portus (Rickman 1971). These were often long ranges of narrow lockable rooms arranged around four sides of a central, colonnaded courtyard, the whole complex effectively sealed off from the outside world by high walls and a limited number of entrance ways. To give some idea of the scale of these structures, the Horrea Galbana (Fig. 43a; cf also Fig. 44a) in Rome covered more than 21,000sq.m (Rickman 1971, 97; 1980, 139, n62). The courtyards were probably used for manoeuvring, sorting and temporarily storing goods although to what extent is uncertain. However, as pressure on space increased in the first century, there was a steady reduction in the amount of space allocated to them in new horrea until eventually they were omitted altogether (Vitelli 1980, 59–60). Simpler linear buildings comprising a range of rooms all opening out on to the same side have been excavated at many har-

42 *Warehouses on the waterfront were probably the focus for a quayside market.*

bours in North Africa (Fig. 43b) and Asia Minor as well as Portus (Rickman 1971, 132; 137). These were also very large and, like the warehouses in Ostia and Portus, were generally, although not exclusively, associated with the grain supply to Rome.

Many provincial cities in the Empire were provided with underground storage areas, called *cryptoportici*, carved out of the rock on which the city was built. They usually comprised long corridors off which lay ranges of narrow rooms, similar in many ways to courtyard horrea. There has been much argument as to whether all these structures should really be interpreted as storage buildings

but it seems certain that some of them – for instance the example at Narbonne – must have been (Gayraud 1981, 247–58; de Ruyt 1983, 333). At the other extreme, many continental horrea were of much simpler design comprising only walled yards for stacking timber etc, or open areas in which great earthenware vessels (*dolia defossa*) were set in the ground and used for storing not only liquids but grain and other solid foodstuffs. Examples of the latter have been identified at Arles (Constans 1921, 336–8), Marseille (Musée d'Histoire de Marseille 1979, 107) as well as Ostia (Rickman 1971, 120).

Storing or selling?

The great differences in plan, form and structure between these types of warehouses seem to be related to the degree to which they functioned

69

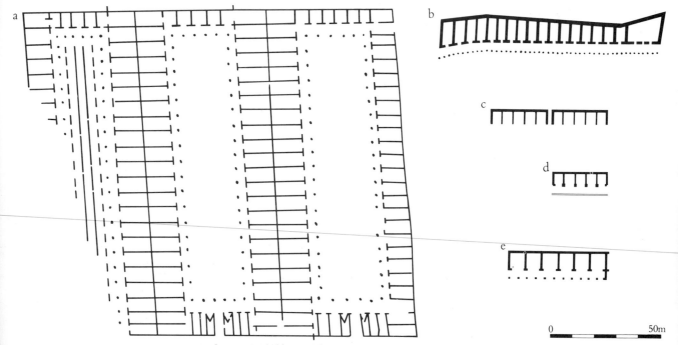

43 *Warehouses and shops. Size and form of:*
a *Horrea Galbana, Rome,*
b *quayside buildings at Leptis Magna, compard with*

c *London's Buildings 1 and 2 in the first century* AD. *Al*
d *plan of shops in Lyons, compared with*
e *London's Buildings 1 and 2 in second century* AD.

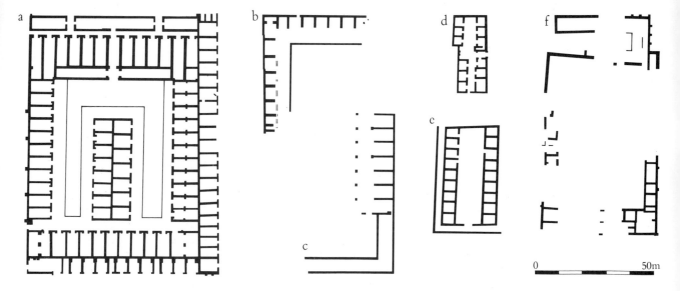

44 *Horrea, Macella or Fora?*
a *Plan of Horrea Grandi, Ostia, showing lockable storerooms inside, shops on outside*
b *shops on inside of Horrea Agripiana, Rome*
c *shops inside forum at Clunia*

d *structure identified as horrea at Ostia*
e *structure identified as macella (market building) at Verulamium*
f *structure identified as first-century forum in London.*

either as mere storehouses or as retail and distribution outlets: ie whether goods were sold or distributed directly from the building as well as being stored there. Three main types of storage may perhaps be suggested. Firstly, long-term storage whether military or civil. Secondly, storage for a shorter period, usually in association with a variety of distribution outlets, such as shops, stalls or markets. Thirdly, the much smaller scale storage facility required by an individual shop or stall, but without any shared or centralised storage space.

At one end of the scale, the massive enclosed warehouses of Rome were designed to store foodstuffs safely for long-term future needs, especially through the winter months when the grain fleets could not sail. Assuring the continuity of the provisioning of Rome, and later other cities like Constantinople, with their enormous parasitic populations ever ready to riot, became a dominant preoccupation for Emperor after Emperor. The quantity and size of warehouses in Rome are adequate testimony to this concern. At the other end of the scale, the *dolia defossa* type of horrea and the underground storage areas have been interpreted by some commentators as the centres for the day-to-day distributive needs of the town, a less permanent form of storage and a role much closer to that of the market (Alzon 1965, 318–25; Rickman 1971, 76).

The possible relationship between storing and selling or distributing can be further developed. For instance, underground storage areas were often located near to and sometimes beneath the forum or main market area with which they presumably functioned. In Ostia some of the courtyard horrea were surrounded by ranges of shops, the storage rooms facing into the courtyard with limited access and the shops facing out onto the street, usually with wide entrances closed off by removable timber shuttering. A study of inscriptions has shown that 'in addition to the *horrearii* on the staff of the Horrea Galbana and other warehouses, there were numbers of people who sold goods of various kinds' (Rickman 1980, 140). It may be suggested therefore that the shops surrounding some of the horrea formed an integral part of the horrea complex. The close relationship of functions is occasionally emphasised by the presence of both within one building. In Rome itself, although the Horrea Agrippiana (Fig. 44b) bore many resemblances to a classic courtyard type warehouse (Figs. 43a and 44a), the ranges of rooms

had no continuous front wall but were closed off by removable wooden shutters like shops (Bauer 1978, figs. 2, 4). Because of this it is argued that its function must have been at least partly that of selling goods (Rickman 1971, 97). Even the distribution of the grain dole in Rome, may, in the absence of any known centralised distributive centre, have been conducted at horrea (Rickman 1980, 185).

Rickman concludes that there is evidence that the warehouses in Rome 'instead of being mere stores and repositories, formed part of a whole pattern of retail trade' (Rickman 1980, 141). This included the *macella*, the riverside *fora*, areas like Trajan's market (*mercatus*) with its 150 shops (*tabernae*) (Cary and Scullard 1975, 467), and the shops that are visible on the Marble Plan of Rome lining virtually every street (Rickman 1980, 141). Even the term *basilica* can have commercial associations: buildings used for the exchange and distribution of cloth, wool etc were known as *basilicae vestiariae* (de Ruyt 1983, 337). It is known that the Romans themselves used different terms, such as *macella*, *fora*, *horrea* etc, for certain building complexes. Although this terminology is perpetuated by present-day archaeologists interpreting the results of excavations, the choice of term is sometimes questionable, and no rigidly defined separation of function should necessarily be assumed. For example, building complexes in Cirencester and Leicester were only identified as *macella* rather than *fora* since the towns in question already had structures thought to be *fora* elsewhere (Wacher 1975, 60). The luxury food market in Rome, although officially called a *macellum*, was known by the populace as the Forum Piscarium, or alternatively the Forum Cuppedenis (de Ruyt 1983, 239). In an important work on *macella*, de Ruyt points out the similarity between the plans of *macella* and some horrea types, but concludes that they had very different functions by drawing attention to the different door and entrance sizes in both building types (de Ruyt 1983, 316; 333). Yet at least one building with wide open-fronted ranges of rooms which was probably involved in selling goods was known as a horrea, as the dedicatory inscription to the Horrea Agrippiana makes clear. Fig. 44 shows the considerable degree of similarity in form and size between buildings named or interpreted variously as *horrea*, *macella* and *fora*. If, as Rickman pointed out, *horrea* had a function that was at least partly that of a market, then it could be argued that some if not many of the rooms ranged around *fora* were for storage. There was almost certainly a considerable degree of overlap in the functions of *macella*, *fora* and some *horrea*, all sharing to differing extents the functions of the market and the warehouse. The greater the provision of easy access, the more a selling or distributive function may be assumed. The more limitations there were on access the more long term security may be assumed to have been the primary objective.

Management and manpower

The question of who was responsible for the initial construction, ownership and subsequent management of warehouses in the provinces is highly complex. In Ostia the pattern from the first century onwards was one of increasing imperial intervention in both ownership and control of warehousing (Vitelli 1980). After the second century, however, it was largely a question of upkeep rather than construction of new horrea. As for other ports, Rickman points out that 'In the provinces it is certain that . . . the upkeep and control of the horrea . . . seem normally to have been the responsibility of the governor (the Emperor's personal representative)' (Rickman 1971, 181). Whether this control was exercised over horrea not connected with the *annona*, the grain supply to Rome, is less certain. Writing specifically about ports other than Ostia and Puteoli, the main Italian ports for the *annona*, one commentator concluded that 'the ordinary administration of Italian ports was left in the hands of local officials, and there was, so far as we can tell, almost no interest in such ports on the part of the central administration during the early Empire' (Houston 1980, 166). Furthermore, it is interesting that even in the massive warehouses under direct imperial control there was provision for 'private subletting'. Individual rooms in these buildings were let out privately for the storage of valuables, rather like safety deposit boxes in banks (Rickman 1971, 5).

Within horrea goods were stored either loose or, more usually, in a variety of sizes of sacks, barrels and amphoras. All of these were unloaded by hand from the ships and lighters in the port. There was virtually no attempt at streamlining or maximising the 'productivity' of the 'dockers'. The ports were highly labour intensive and must have been a hive of activity. 'The cargoes were laboriously unloaded by countless porters, the *sacarii*, who ran along the gang-planks laid from the prows of the ships to the quaysides and humped either bundles, or sacks of produce, or amphorae of wine and oil on their backs' (Rickman 1971, 8). There was generally very little provision for the use of carts in the whole system – it was all designed around manpower. In fact this is only half the story: in Rome, goods which arrived at the quayside had already been transferred from the deep-water seagoing vessels to smaller lighters called *naves codicariae* – a highly time-consuming process (Casson 1965; see Chapter 9). It is possible that the work was performed not by slaves but by the poor 'earning their living in casual employment . . . in the unloading and porterage of goods that arrived by sea' (Brunt 1980, 81). If such were also the case in Roman London, the labour intensive activity of the harbour would have provided some work for the town's poorer inhabitants.

The confusion along the quayside must have been made worse by the presence of people buying directly from the ships and warehouses. It was not only traders but 'ordinary townsfolk', buying in relatively small quantities, who came to the waterfront. 'The docks were thus a magnet for many different kinds of people including quite ordinary inhabitants of Rome, in a way totally unlike the commercial docks of the modern world' (Rickman 1971, 9). The harbour area itself is therefore also to be seen as part of a general market pattern which included *horrea*, *fora* and *macella*.

Markets and storage in London

It is possible to identify at least two separate areas of storage and selling in Roman London. Firstly a strip along the quayside comprising buildings for temporary storage and at least a small market area, that is the two large buildings erected to the north of the late first-century quay, labelled 1 and 2 on Figs. 13 and 14c. These almost certainly replaced earlier timber warehouses in a similar location (Fig. 14b). Upstream of the bridge the existence of another warehouse has been argued from marked concentrations of samian pottery. Further upstream part of a building at the Miles Lane site may at some period have been in use as a warehouse.

Secondly the area around and including the forum on the crest of the city's eastern hill, comprising buildings for longer-term as well as short-term storage and a major market area. The forum itself may, as suggested earlier, have had a function that was at least partly that of a warehouse. These areas or possible groups of buildings will now be examined in greater detail.

Pl. 1 *Part of London's late first-century harbour, looking north, at high tide. The water laps up against the timber-faced quay (2 x 100mm scale) and fills part of an open drain. The 0.5m scale rests on the* compacted working surface which leads into the westernmost bay of an open-fronted waterfront warehouse (Building 2), the walls of which survive over 1m in height.

Pl. 2a *Samian stamps from the Pudding Lane site. The commonest stamps were those of the first-century potter Passienus from La Graufesenque, seen at the top. Beneath, on the outside of a vessel, is a stamp of CIN(namus), a potter who worked in the late second century.*

Pl. 2b *Beakers with characteristic shapes and decorations can be dated with some accuracy.* **From left to right:** *locally-made beaker, mid- to late first century; 'poppy-head' beaker from Highgate, early second century; hunt beaker from Cologne, late second century; indented beaker from Moselle, late second century; Nene Valley indented beaker, late third to fourth century.*

As, Claudius, irregular copy,
copper, AD 43-60

Dupondius, Vespasian,
orichalcum (brass), AD 72

Sestertius, Vespasian,
orichalcum, AD 77-8

Denarius, Trajan, silver,
AD 112-4

Antoninianus, 'radiate',
Gordian III, copper silver-
washed, AD 241-3

Antoninianus, 'radiate',
Tacitus. copper silver-
washed, AD 275-6

Urbs Roma, Trier mint,
copper, AD 330-5

Siliqua, Valentinian I, Rome
mint, silver, AD 364-7

Valentinian I, Aquileia mint,
copper, AD 367-75

Pl. 3 *The changing face of coinage from the London waterfront.*

Pl. 4a *The south west corner of the late first-century quay (0.5m scale) with the north wall of the possible bridge pier base in the open river to the south.*

Pl. 4b *General view of the eastern quay in the late first century recorded near Fish Street Hill, looking north, away from the river. The infill deposits have been excavated to east and west of the 1m scale revealing braces, earlier features, and the foundations of the waterfront warehouse Building 1 in the east.*

Pl. 5a *Part of the open-fronted waterfront* horrea *(Building 2) with 1m scale against its north wall, recorded just west of Pudding Lane in 1981; note burnt timber floor.*

Pl. 5b *Apsidal-ended bath in Building 6 faced with white tesserae with red band over quarter-round moulding on which 2 x 100mm scale rests.*

Pl. 6a *Coloured stones from Gaul, the eastern Mediterranean and Egypt used as inlays and mouldings in Roman London.*
Left hand group: *black and white marble from Aquitaine;* campan vert *from the Pyrenees; black carboniferous limestone, probably from north east Gaul.*
Top right hand group: Cipollino *from Euboea, Greece; white marble with blue/grey veining from the Aegean or western Turkey; green porphyry from Sparta;* portasanta *from Chios;* pavonazzetto *from Phrygia;* semesanto *from Skyros.*
Bottom right hand group: *Greenish-grey gabbro or dolerite, black and white diorite, red porphyry, all from eastern Egypt.*

Pl. 6b *In the first and second centuries, glass vessels of many different types were imported into London.*
Back row, left to right: *small flask, tall ribbed flagon, pillar-moulded bowl, common square storage bottle.*
Middle row: *jar with string rim, flat rimmed jar, mould blown beaker.*
Front row: *two-handled cup (*skyphos*).*

Pl. 7a *Part of the large consignment of unused imported pottery found near the third-century quay on the St Magnus House site. The vessels came from Rheinzabem and Trier in Germany and Lezoux in France.*

Pl. 7b *Roman lamps.* **From left to right:** *volute lamp decorated with laurel wreath, from Lyon, first century; plain-nozzled lamp, possibly from southern Gaul, late first or early second century; samian ware and black-slipped 'factory' lamps from Lezoux, mid to late second century; mica-dusted factory 'lamp' and open lamp from Verulamium region, late first or second century.*

Pl. 8a *In the second century, the southern room in Building 6 incorporated a latrine (0.5m scale) which disgorged westwards into a main drain at top of picture.*

Pl. 8b *The southern room of Building 6 in the third century, with 0.5m scale to south, showing doorway and mosaic floor discoloured by later addition of hypocaust; see Pl. 8c.*

Pl. 8c *In the late fourth century, Building 6 rebuilt and hypocaust added (2 x 100mm scale). Compare Pl. 8b.*

THE WATERFRONT AREA: BUILDINGS 1 AND 2

Buildings 1 and 2 (Pls. 1, 5a; Figs. 14c, 45a, 79) were each c25m long and 6m wide, set parallel to the river, and were apparently divided up into five bays c4.3m wide. Each bay contained a timber floor at c+2.25m OD – slightly higher than the top of the timber quay – comprising planking laid on regularly spaced timber joists which were themselves raised above ground level on rows of piles. The internal faces of the masonry walls were rendered with rough pink plaster which was continued down over the edge of the timber floor as a quarter-round moulding. Since the north, east and west walls of each building survived up to 1.5m above the level of the timber floor it is assumed that the regular courses of ragstone with tile bonding courses continued all the way to the eaves. By contrast, the substantial foundations which separated the bays in each building were deliberately capped with a thick layer of mortar at the same height as the timber floors on either side of them. It is uncertain whether the partitions which were built over these foundations were 'solid' with no access between adjacent bays, or 'open', perhaps utilising a series of timber columns. It certainly seems unlikely that the partitions were masonry. The roofs of both buildings were tiled: both buildings were later badly damaged by fire and the burnt planks of the timber floor were sealed by a thick layer of charred timbers and roof tiles.

Although in some respects the two buildings were identical, there were differences in the form of their southern walls, the side facing onto the quay. For example on the south side of Building 1 was a substantial sub-surface foundation, the top of which was sealed with two courses of bonding tile at the same height as the brickearth and gravel surface to the south. The charred remains of a timber on this foundation may represent a cill-beam, although no evidence survived of the superstructure it presumably supported. It would therefore seem that, unlike the other external walls, the south wall was not carried to the eaves in masonry.

The south-facing frontage of Building 2 was very different: instead of a masonry foundation it had a narrow vertical-sided gully or trench along the bottom and sides of which were traces of timber planking. This is interpreted as a drainage gully, although it is also conceivable that the trench represents a robbed timber cill-beam slot.

In spite of these differences in form, it is likely that both frontages were designed to serve a similar purpose, namely the provision of open and easy access from the quayside to the internal bays of both buildings. It is suggested that removable timber shuttering could have been used to close each individual bay, as in shops or the Horrea Agrippiana.

Both buildings are best interpreted as storage buildings, since they were almost certainly built at the same time as the quay onto which they opened, suggesting that their function may also have been directly related to it. An interesting point, however, is the degree to which they differ from known harbourside storage buildings elsewhere in the Empire. As strip buildings with rows of rooms all facing out onto the contemporary quayside they in some ways resemble the buildings at Leptis Magna (see Fig. 43b). However, the absence of any solid masonry front wall in the London buildings is a significant difference: as suggested above, they may well have been closed off by removable shutters like the Horrea Agrippiana. Although the timber floors of the London buildings were raised on piles, like the floors of some kinds of military granaries, there were no openings for ventilation through the masonry walls – a feature otherwise invariably associated with raised floors – nor were the walls buttressed. In addition the buildings do not seem to have been divided up into separate, mutually inaccessible rooms, as were the courtyard warehouses in Rome or granaries in Britannia. Instead it seems that rows of free standing timber columns may have supported the roof, leaving an essentially open floor space of 150sq.m in each building (Bateman and Milne 1983, 217). Open-area warehouses with roofs supported by internal columns are known at Trier and Veldidena (Rickman 1971, 264–6).

The small scale of the London warehouses is striking when compared with even the Leptis Magna building, quite apart from one of the larger warehouses of Rome. Buildings 1 and 2 had a combined floor space of c300sq.m: at Leptis Magna just one of the warehouses had a floor space of c700sq.m. Although the population of London has been estimated as 30,000 (Frere 1967, 267) some twenty times smaller than that of Rome, Buildings 1 and 2 together were as much as seventy times smaller than the Horrea Galbana which was only one of many in Rome. The *Notitia Regionum XIV* of AD 354 records a total of 290 horrea, thirty-five of the largest of which were in the Aventine, the harbour area (Rickman 1971, 323). Some comparison with military warehouses is also illuminating.

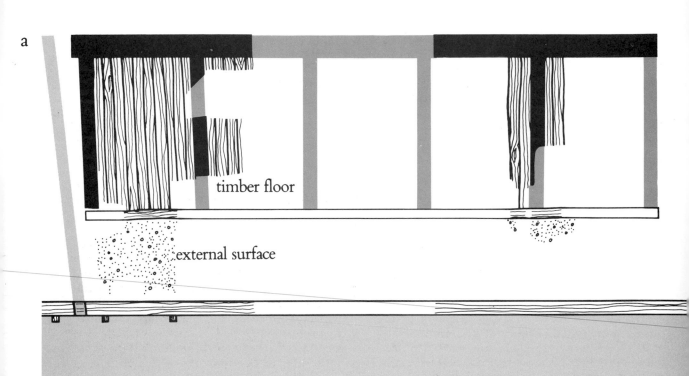

a

timber floor

external surface

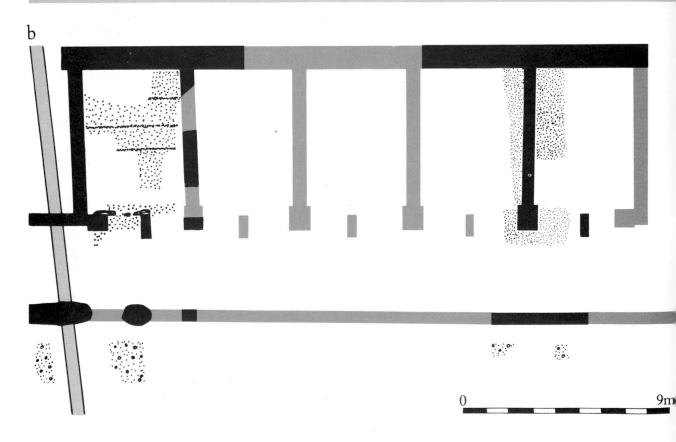

b

0   9m

Each of the six granaries in the legionary fortress at Inchtuthil in Scotland (Rickman 1971, 220) had a floor space of over 500sq.m yet these storebuildings contained the supplies for only 5000–6000 men. Of perhaps greater interest is the fact that in addition to the six granaries identified at Inchtuthil, the main axial streets in the fortress were lined on both sides with ranges of open-fronted rooms, interpreted by the excavator as offices or subsidiary store rooms, which were very similar in form and dimension to Buildings 1 and 2 in London (*JRS* 1960, 160). This would appear to give the fortress a storage capacity far in excess of its needs and it may be that this kind of open-fronted range was a plan-form adaptable to many different functions, from shops to *horrea* to offices.

Observations on form, considered in conjunction with the enormous discrepancy in size between the London buildings and the warehouses of Rome and the Mediterranean ports, suggest that Buildings 1 and 2 should not be interpreted as granaries, or indeed as any form of long-term food storage buildings, where the storage of bulk provisions for resident populations, civil or military, was the primary need. Given the relative lack of security, it is probable that the buildings were initially only used for temporary storage, somewhat like transit sheds in the nineteenth-century docks.

It is not known what specific types of merchandise were accommodated in the buildings, since no artefacts was found in direct association with them; indeed when the buildings were destroyed by fire in the early to mid-second century, they were apparently completely empty. It is interesting to speculate whether this was due to deliberate clearance in advance of a fire before which there was some time for preparation, or because the buildings were frequently empty. Perhaps they were burnt in the winter when ships were not sailing, and the buildings were therefore unused. However, some idea of the kind of goods which may have been stored there can be derived from the frequent barrel and amphora remains found in the quay infill dumps and the foreshores which built up against the quays. Merchandise included wine, olive oil, *garum*, pottery, dates, and fish. These are discussed at greater length in Chapter 10.

45 *Building 2, initially constructed as a London waterfront horrea or warehouse.*
a *late first century* b *second century.*

The buildings were extended but otherwise not greatly modified after the next major phase of land reclamation in the early second century, but stopped functioning as warehouses after a destructive fire some twenty-five years later. The subsequent rebuilding saw significant changes in form, including the introduction of a series of solid masonry walls over the foundations of the earlier partitions, at the southern ends of which rectangular piers or buttresses of coursed tile were constructed. This significantly altered the southern frontage, and presumably also the function of the building: one of the closest parallels to the new form of the buildings is a series of shops in Lyon (Audin 1972) built on high ground well away from the waterfront area (Fig. 43). The connections between selling and storage have already been discussed and it may be suggested that the London buildings, which were originally designed with the combined functions of shops and warehouses, were converted to a more easily recognisable shop form as the working waterfront was advanced, and replacement horrea were built (see Chapter 2).

THE WATERFRONT AREA: OTHER BUILDINGS

Evidence for the latter was found to the south of Buildings 1 and 2 where new masonry walls were constructed after the mid-second-century fire (Building 9; Fig. 17a). Unfortunately, no associated floor surfaces survived. The walls, which were recorded in two widely separated trenches, were parallel to the new quay, but at a distinctly different angle to that of Buildings 1 and 2. The features are thought to represent the north wall of a range of replacement storage buildings. They may have initially housed the samian pottery which was subsequently cleared and discarded in bulk in the infill dumps of a quay erected just to the south in the early third century (see Chapter 2). These masonry buildings seem to have replaced Building 4 (Fig 14d) and several other mud-brick structures represented by a 1m thick layer of redeposited fire debris from which an iron window grille was recovered (Fig. 46).

Traces of a much larger structure were also recorded to the south of Buildings 1 and 2, presumably representing a building which, in the fourth century, replaced the possible 'samian store' described above. All that survived was a series of regularly spaced T-shaped piers or buttresses. These cannot have been integrated with the buildings to the north (Bateman and Milne 1983, 221) and may therefore have formed part of the portico

46 *Reconstruction of an iron window grille used in a mud brick waterfront building destroyed in a mid-second-century fire. The fragments which survived are shown in the darker tone. Drawn by N. Griffiths.*

of a large structure to the south (Building 5; Fig. 17e). Its apparent size could suggest that it was not a domestic structure, and it may have served a commercial function, perhaps as another horrea.

The bulk of waterfront warehousing might be expected to lie in the area east of the bridge, the structure of which would have impeded the progress of river traffic moving upstream. Indeed, the level of the artificial waterfront terrace laid out in the first century was up to 1m higher on the upstream side where it was examined on the Miles Lane site (Miller 1982). This substantial difference would have made it more difficult to unload cargoes from boats moored against the quay. However, some evidence for storage facilities has been recorded in this area. The recent excavations revealed a 9m wide building aligned at right angles to the quay (Building A; Figs. 12, 14b). It was set 2m behind the quay front and extended at least 36m northwards with four rooms rising in terraces up the hillside (Miller 1982). The walls were 0.65m wide, built of ragstone with tile bonding courses, and survived up to 1m above the contemporary floor surfaces. The southern wall, however, did not extend above floor level and was sealed by a mortar surface, suggesting that the building was open-fronted. The southern room was much larger than the other rooms and had a particularly solid and well-constructed floor of thick concrete. The floors in the other rooms were generally less substantial, possibly suggesting a different function. Under the floors of the two southern rooms, a brick-lined culvert ran down towards the river. The terrace walls dividing the rooms were vaulted to allow the passage of this culvert and it emerged from the front of the building to empty into a sump box from which it was piped out to the river itself. The apparently open front of the southern room might suggest use as a storage building with the mid-first-century quay immediately to its south. However, with the possible exception of this most southerly room, the excavator concludes that the rest of the building was unlikely to have been used for storage (Miller 1982, 147).

Clearer evidence for the existence of a warehouse close to the bridge is provided by another large concentration of samian pottery (Marsh 1981). This assemblage was discovered in the 1920s on the Regis House site (Fig. 14d) and had been badly burnt in a second-century fire. The exact position of the storehouse itself is not known, since the pottery was mixed with a massive dump of redeposited burnt mud-brick debris. Nevertheless, the sheer quantity of samian ware from the one site suggests that the associated horrea cannot have been too far away.

No other structures similar to Buildings 1 and 2 have been revealed in recent waterfront excavations. It seems that neither the quay nor the warehouses behind it extended as far as the Billingsgate Building excavation (Fig. 9). Since at present there is therefore little evidence to suggest the existence of other warehouses in the first-century waterfront area, it seems possible that Buildings 1 and 2 could represent a significant proportion of the goods-handling facilities of the contemporary port. Certainly their position immediately downstream of the bridge but adjacent to the main north-south access road to the forum, suggests that they could have been the most important.

From comparison with other known horrea types it seems unlikely that these London warehouses were associated with long-term storage or bulk storage of foodstuffs. They may possibly be seen as buildings in which relatively small quantities of imported merchandise or outward-bound goods could be temporarily stored, checked or repackaged as required. Subsequently the merchandise could have been distributed directly from the buildings themselves or transferred for longer-term storage to other buildings away from the waterfront, possibly in the forum area.

THE FORUM AREA

The area around the forum some 300m to the north of the waterfront may have been the centre for longer-term storage of certain goods and their subsequent distribution (Fig. 8). For example, Merrifield suggested that a small building found near Fenchurch Street (just south of the forum) in 1923 might have been a granary (Merrifield 1965, 291); Marsden suggested that if it was, it may have been associated with the storage of grain arriving from the surrounding countryside rather than from the harbour (Marsden 1980, 72).

It is possible that the forum itself, or at least some of its rooms, may have been used for long-term storage. As already pointed out, there is a definite similarity in form between certain *fora* and *horrea* as well as a potential overlap of function. No agreement has been reached on the function of the large masonry building which preceded the second-century forum in London. Indeed, there is even a measure of doubt as to whether only a single unified structure is represented. Although it has been tentatively labelled a 'proto forum' by some (Philp 1977) and identified as a forum by others (Marsden 1978), it seems equally possible that it could have been called a *macella* or a *horrea*. In plan form it is very similar to many of the courtyard horrea described by Rickman and the existence of substantial buttresses round several of the external walls may also be significant.

It is conceivable that the area on the top of the eastern hill had always been used for certain types of bulk storage. For instance, in one of the timber buildings which underlay the forum and had been burnt in the Boudican revolt, a deposit of burnt grain over 1m thick was found (Straker 1984). Although the structure associated with the grain has been interpreted as a shop (Marsden 1980, 33), the deposit does seem unusually thick and a longer-term storage building may in fact be indicated. The grain was almost certainly imported, suggesting that at this relatively early date self-sufficiency had not yet been achieved. More recently, substantial deposits of burnt grain were identified on another site to the south-east of the forum. Skeletal remains of the black rat (*Rattus rattus*) were identified in the backfill of a nearby well and it is suggested that the presence of both grain and rats on the same site should not be seen as coincidental. The forum and basilica 'were surrounded by the highest concentration of settlement, including shops and warehouses containing stored food products; all of which would have formed an ideal environment for infestation by rats and mice' (Armitage *et al* 1984, 377).

Conclusions

At least two views can be taken of the relationship of the two possible market/warehouse areas. It is possible that the main distinction in function between the areas lay in the provenance of the goods which they dealt with: the waterfront market handling imported river-borne goods and the forum area handling produce and goods brought in by road from the surrounding country. However, the two areas cannot have been totally mutually exclusive since it is known that imported grain – which must have arrived at the waterfront – was stored up in the forum area.

The alternative view is that the distinction in function between the two areas was primarily one of length of storage: short-term storage and a minor market associated with the waterfront and long-term storage and the main market area associated with the forum.

In both cases it seems likely that the waterfront buildings were primarily associated with the storing and selling of relatively small quantities of the kind of luxury goods for which we have evidence in the form of amphora sherds – wine, *garum*, olive-oil etc (see Chapter 10). One recent survey concluded that 'Londinium was a large and busy port, probably handling more tonnage than any other port in Roman Europe' (Morris 1982, 162). This interpretation is not supported by the archaeological evidence. The waterfront development as a whole was certainly extensive, incorporating massive timber revetments. Nevertheless, the relatively modest scale of the waterfront horrea is surely significant, given their favourable location in the heart of the harbour, since the scale of an ancient port's storage facilities should directly reflect the scale of the associated traffic.

CHAPTER 7

THE ROMAN RIVER

Rising river levels

The GLC's Thames Barrier was officially opened in 1984, to relieve Londoners of the threat of flooding from exceptional high tides. However, not even that remarkable feat of engineering can save the City from a longer-term problem, that of the inexorable rise of the general level of the Thames, or, more correctly, of the sea relative to south-east England. Considerable debate and speculation has been generated by those seeking the causes of such changes (Everard 1980, 1–15; Greensmith and Tooley 1982), and those attempting to calculate what the rate of change was, is, and – of especial importance – will be.

The subject is the archetypal multi-disciplinary study, with a large and ever-increasing quantity of literature 'scattered among the works of astronomers, geophysicists, geologists, geomorphologists, hydrographers, oceanographers, climatologists, biologists, archaeologists, historians, land surveyors, civil engineers, etc. The list amply emphasises the very complex interdependence of the dynamics of the solid earth, the world ocean, and the atmosphere' (Everard 1980, 1). The complexities have been clearly and comprehensively summarised in Everard's lucid paper which appeared in the Society of Antiquaries' *Archaeology and Coastal Change* report (Thompson 1980), required reading for anyone interested in the subject in general.

Archaeologists working in the City can make a positive contribution to the study by correctly identifying, dating, and calculating the level of horizons and features related to the position of the ancient river. Once the changes in the level of the Thames at various historic periods have been established and plotted on a graph, then the rate of change in the past can be calculated and ultimately, the rate of change in the future predicted.

However, before the results of recent work are summarised, the terminology and methods of measurement used should be outlined. Today, the level of the Thames fluctuates continuously, like all tidal rivers, changing from high water to low water in just over six hours. Moreover, the level of water at high (or low) tide varies from week to week. For example, the highest present-day astronomical tide (a calculation which does not take into account the effects of drought or exceptional rainfall etc) would be some 7.7m above the level of the lowest astronomical tide, but is anticipated only eight times a year. The tides which occur after each full or new moon are known as the Spring Tides, and those which follow the moon's first or third quarter are the Neaps. The highest Springs are higher than the highest Neaps; the lowest Springs are lower than the lowest Neaps.

Until recently, there was a tendency 'for land surveyors to assume a stable sea level against which they could measure coastal change, and for hydrographers to assume a stable land against which they could compare sea-level movements'. Unfortunately the stability of neither can be assumed (Everard 1980, 3). The levels in this report are all related to Ordnance Datum (OD), the Mean Sea Level calculated by the Ordnance Survey at Newlyn in Cornwall from observations made since 1915. However, a better reference level for calculating Mean Sea Level movements in Europe during the last 15,000 years may be the *Normaal Amsterdam Peil* (NAP), since records of Mean Sea Level have been kept in Amsterdam since 1682. NAP is the zero for the Unified European Levelling Network (UELN). Port of London Authority and Admiralty charts calculate water levels relative to a Chart Datum, a figure which coincides approximately with the level of the Lowest Astronomical Tide, which varies from place to place. Trinity High Water (THW) on the other hand, is taken as being at +3.475m OD, and approximates to a Mean High Water level at London Bridge. Neither of these measures is appropriate for the calculation of ancient water levels.

Background to the study

The level of the River Thames relative to the land

47 *Old Father Thames. This white Carrara marble head of a Roman river god, possibly a personification of the Thames, was found in the Walbrook valley c1889.*

has been subject to continuous and considerable change over at least the last 10,000 years. This was, and still is, a result of changes in sea-level (eustatic change) as well as uplift and subsidence (tectonic or isostatic change) of the land. A significant factor responsible for changes in sea-level relative to the land in the temperate zones of the northern hemisphere was eustatic rise largely brought about when great quantities of ice began melting after the last glaciation 10,000–14,000 years ago. During this period there were also changes in level of the land relative to that of the sea. For example, there was subsidence in part of the North Sea Basin

including the Thames estuary and south-east England (West 1972, 87; Dunham 1972, 81–6; Devoy 1979, 393; D'Olier 1972, 121–30). This situation is further complicated by the fact that factors influencing sea-level change and subsidence are all potentially interactive. However, it is possible to measure net change. Across most of the London Basin, compensatory isostatic uplift has occurred in association with subsidence throughout the post-glacial period: the inland areas show net uplift; the coastal areas net subsidence.

Recent work by Devoy has added to our knowledge of these changes in the Thames estuary (Devoy 1977, 712–5; 1979, 355–407; 1980, 134–48). A study was made of post-glacial deposits exposed in the estuary between Crossness and the Isle of Grain, and the heights of relative sea-level movements calculated from this work. By plotting these values against time, the rate of sea-level change relative to the land in south-east England was tabulated and compared with evidence from south-west England. As a result Devoy (1979, 348) tentatively suggested that south-east England had subsided 2 to 3 metres relative to the south-west in the last 10,000 years, while the sea-level had risen by more than 25 metres over the same period.

The relative increase in sea-level is not, however, a smooth progression but appears to involve five marine transgressions (periods of sea-level rise) and five phases of regression (periods when the sea-level dropped). The transgressions are indicated by deposits of inorganic muds with silt and clay-size particles. The regressions are recognised in a series of biogenic deposits including peats representing the decayed remains of such material as riverside marsh plants. Radiocarbon dates for the changes were obtained from samples at the point of contact between the transgression and regression deposits. The five regressive phases were identified at Tilbury, and are therefore termed Tilbury I to V.

This chapter is primarily concerned with the period before the latest of these events: the transgression marked by sea-level reaching +0.4m OD at Tilbury in cAD 200. Subsequently, the Tilbury V regression occurred, represented by a thin silty peat at this level (Devoy 1979, 391). This could suggest that during the first and second centuries AD, the river was approaching its maximum level in London before the onset of the Tilbury V regression (Fig. 50). But these data for the transgressions and regressions were collected outside the City reach, and the results cannot therefore be directly related to areas upstream. As an added complication, the course of the Thames has also changed, as Nunn's study of the river in central London during the post-glacial period has demonstrated (Nunn 1983). This paper is of especial importance to London archaeologists since it suggests that the channel of the Thames migrated northwards in a series of stages over the last 10,000 years. It is argued that, from the mesolithic to the early Iron Age, the course of the Thames lay to the south of its present-day position, by as much as 3km at the beginning of this period.

Clearly, with such profound changes in the course and level of the Thames, the position of the tidal head of the river must also have fluctuated. Analysis of microscopic unicellular algae, known as diatoms, from sites in the Thames estuary (Devoy 1977, 1979, 1980) indicates an early and increasing degree of salinity in the post-glacial period, and implies movement of the tidal limit upstream towards London. Dr Akeroyd claimed that freshwater conditions prevailed not only at London, but as far downstream as Dagenham and Crossness in the Roman period (Akeroyd 1972, 155). Her position was cautiously supported by Willcox in a paper which was accorded general acceptance (Willcox 1975), at least by archaeologists working in the City (eg Marsden 1980, 12). However, the new evidence from excavations on both banks of the Thames allows first-century river levels to be fixed more confidently and demonstrates that, contrary to the accepted view, the River Thames in Roman London was tidal.

The south bank in the first century

The detailed published evidence both for the topography of the south bank and for a river level at $c + 1$m OD in the mid-first century (Graham 1978) was recently updated by Brian Yule (Milne, Battarbee, Straker and Yule 1983), from which paper the following paragraph was compiled. It seems that the river flowed as much as 700m south of the modern Southwark waterfront along braided channels intersecting islands of relatively high ground (but mostly below $+ 1.5$m OD) and mud flats. Roads providing access to London were constructed in AD 50–55 across this very marginal ground (Graham 1978, fig. 4). The estimation of river levels was based on the original tops of first-century revetments, and on the heights of water-laid deposits, which are difficult to relate to actual river levels. Nevertheless, with the exception of two sites (Graham 1978, 239; Denis forthcoming)

there is no evidence for flooding subsequent to road construction. In the absence of proven Roman flood defences protecting the southern approach roads to London, the evidence indicates that the river level was not expected to exceed $+ 1.50$m, the height of the lowest operative road surfaces.

The north bank in the first century

The excavation of the late first-century quay surviving to its full height provided clear evidence for the level of the Roman river (Pl. 1; Fig. 48). A gravel bank c0.8m high with its top at $c + 1.6$m OD was also found on the Pudding Lane site, to the north of the quay mentioned above. It had been raised earlier than the quay, whose infilling deposits sealed it. It was aligned east-west on the southern edge of what had originally been the 'natural' north bank of the Thames, over 100m north of the present river channel. On an adjacent site, a post and plank revetment was recorded 15m to the east of the bank but on the same alignment, the surviving top of which was at $c + 1.7$m OD. It too was earlier than the late first-century quay, and both bank and revetment are interpreted as part of an early Roman attempt to strengthen and straighten the river-bank, and to curb flooding up to a level of $c + 1.6$m OD (Fig. 14a).

The construction of the timber-faced quay found on the Pudding Lane site has been dated to the late first century. Sandy waterlaid deposits had accumulated up against its south face and were also found to the north of it, showing that the structure had been built out over the foreshore into the open Roman river (Fig. 48). The analysis of these foreshore sediments is discussed below. The base plates were laid at c Ordnance Datum, and the original top of the structure survived at $c + 2$m OD, approximately level with the contemporary working surface to the north. It is argued that when this structure was built and these surfaces were laid, the river was not expected to rise above $+ 2$m OD. A mean high water level somewhere between $+ 1$ and $+ 1.5$m OD in the mid-first century would therefore be consistent with the structural evidence from the Pudding Lane site. This also agrees with the evidence from Southwark.

Evidence for a tidal Roman river

The evidence that the River Thames was tidal in the early Roman period is based on both archaeological and palaeoecological data. Excavators on the Miles Lane and Pudding Lane sites found clay

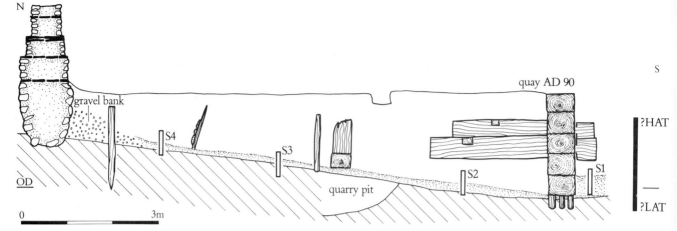

N

quay AD 90

S

gravel bank

?HAT

S4

S3

OD

quarry pit

S2

S1

?LAT

0   3m

48 *Measured north-south section across the Roman waterfront showing quarry pit beneath late first-century quay and working surfaces on quayside. Suggested levels of the Highest and Lowest Astronomical Tides are marked, together with the position of Samples 1–4, taken for diatom analysis.*

quarry pits on the foreshore. At Miles Lane (Miller 1982, 143–4) a pit 12m by 9m had been cut from Ordnance Datum to a depth of −1.28m OD. At Pudding Lane, a much smaller pit at least 1.5m in diameter had been dug into the London Clay at Ordnance Datum to a depth of −0.8m (Figs. 14a, 48). Pottery from the fill of the pits showed that they had been exposed – and presumably dug – in the first century AD. Although it has already been argued that the contemporary river must have risen to a height of between + 1m and + 1.5m OD, it must also have receded below Ordnance Datum in this period to permit quarrying. Such a fluctuating level suggests that the river was tidal, and had a tidal range (amplitude) in excess of 1.5m.

Diatom analysis of the first-century foreshore sediments by Dr Battarbee confirms this inference (Battarbee 1983; Milne, Battarbee, Straker and Yule 1983). Four column samples up to 560mm in height were taken from the foreshores exposed on the Pudding Lane site, to the north and south of the late first-century quay (S1 to S4 on Fig. 48). The foreshore sediments themselves varied from 420mm thick in Sample 1 to 100mm thick in Sample 3. These sediments were sub-sampled for diatom analysis prepared at 40mm intervals using standard procedures (Battarbee 1979). Results from the analysis of Sample 1 were not significantly different from those from Sample 2. The dominant species at all levels was the brackish

water-loving species *Cylotella striata*, a very common planktonic diatom in European river estuaries (Hustedt 1957). It occurs in the contemporary Thames, and has been found in other early sediments of the river including deposits on the Swan Lane site to the south of Thames Street (Battarbee, unpublished) and the medieval sediment from the River Fleet (Boyd 1981). In the Pudding Lane material it is exceptionally well preserved, which, together with its numerical dominance, suggests that it was derived directly from the adjacent river. Other brackish forms include *Nitzschia sigma*, *Synedra tabulata var. affinis* and *Bacillaria paradoxa*.

There is a small number of marine species in the sediments such as *Cymatosira belgica*, *Raphoneis surirella*, *R. amphiceros* and *Cocconeis scutellum*. These are infrequent and either small forms or small fragments, but nevertheless they demonstrate the tidal nature of the river.

The majority of the species in the assemblages are freshwater forms, although many of the dominants, such as *Fragilaria pinnata*, *Surirella ovata*, *Cocconeis placentula*, are often also found in weakly brackish environments. Consequently they could have been growing close to the site of deposition. Other freshwater forms are likely to have been carried down the river from sites upstream above the tidal head. No freshwater plankton was observed.

The palaeoecological analysis clearly demonstrates that in the first century, when the sampled foreshore sediments were accumulating, the river adjacent to the Pudding Lane site was estuarine, ie it was influenced by tides. It is difficult to estimate likely salinities of the water with accuracy, although the Pudding Lane spectrum, with 2 per cent marine forms, is less saline than that from the

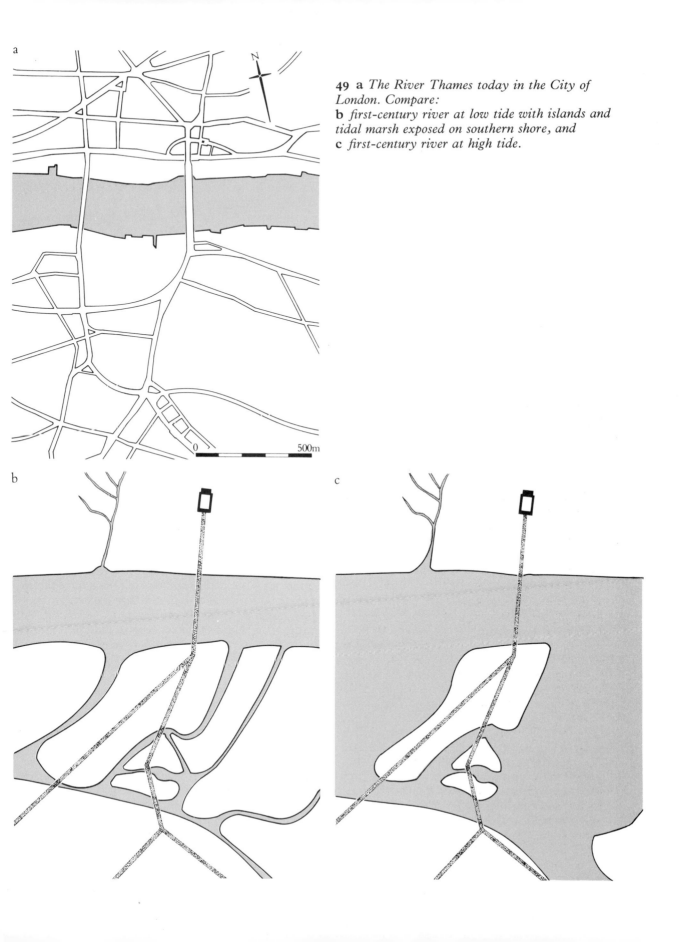

49 a *The River Thames today in the City of London. Compare:*
b *first-century river at low tide with islands and tidal marsh exposed on southern shore, and*
c *first-century river at high tide.*

early medieval Swan Lane site, where 11 per cent of the assemblage was marine. This may indicate that the tidal head of the river was closer to the City in the first century than in the medieval period.

Riverside topography

The structural, stratigraphic and environmental evidence from first-century sites in London on both banks is consistent with the suggestions that the contemporary Thames was tidal and regularly reached a height of at least +1.25m OD. It was not expected to rise above c+1.8m to +2m OD, but receded below Ordnance Datum, and thus had a tidal amplitude of at least c1.5m. The figures of +1.25m OD and Ordnance Datum do not represent the highest and lowest tides, or Mean High and Mean Low Water, or any other specific water level, but are levels which, it can be argued, the Roman river attained, but almost certainly exceeded. The figures for the highest and lowest first-century tides as yet identified do not represent as broad a range as those suggested for the fourteenth century (Milne and Milne 1982, 60–62), and are considerably less than the present-day values (PLA 1983).

If it is accepted that the first-century tidal river attained at least the levels suggested, then the width of the river during high and low tides can be calculated by plotting the 1.25 and 0m contours for both banks, as on Fig. 49. Though this exercise does not depict the situation at the highest and lowest tides, it suggests that the river may have been up to 1km wide (including marshland) at high tide to the south of Roman London. At low tide, it would have decreased to c275m wide at its narrowest point, substantially wider than the present day channel which is c200m across.

Although Figs. 49b and 49c represent a change in river level of only 1.25m, the effect of even this modest tidal range on the topography of the south bank is dramatic. Clearly much of the foreshore was inter-tidal marsh land, a situation recalling the description by Cassius Dio which may refer to the London area during the advance of the Roman army in AD 43:

> Thence the Britons retired to the River Thames at a point near where it . . . at flood tide forms a lake. This they easily crossed because they knew where the firm ground . . . (was) . . . to be found. . . . But the Romans . . . got into swamps from which it was difficult to make their way out, and so lost a number of men. (*RCHM* 1928, 2)

The problems facing the Roman engineers who considered bridging the Thames in cAD 50, and the crucial importance of the 'islands' on the southern shore to that project are obvious. The narrowest part of the river was east of the tributary River Walbrook, north of the largest southern 'island' (assuming that there were no other islands in midstream), a distance of c300m in the first century. This point is due south of the first-century timber feature recorded on the Pudding Lane site just east of Fish Street Hill (Milne 1982), thought to represent a pier-base for an early timber bridge.

The first bridge over the Thames was a major road crossing, at both ends of which settlements developed. Of these, the northern one was destined to become the more important, a reflection of the unfavourable natural topography to the south: nevertheless it was precisely because dry land was so limited on the southern shore that Southwark's topography dictated where the roads, the bridge – and therefore the City itself – would be built.

The late Roman river

On Fig. 50 columns displaying the suggested tidal range in the first and fourteenth centuries and one showing the present day values have been plotted against curves for Mean Sea Level and Mean High Water Spring Tides in the outer and inner estuary respectively. Although the basis on which the information was gathered is different in each case, some general statements are possible. The pattern of the changing water level exhibited in the inner and outer estuary curves is broadly similar (with the noteworthy exception of the most modern data) although the outer estuary readings are more exaggerated. The suggested difference in the absolute heights of the two curves is to be expected: present day Highest Astronomical Tide at Tilbury (inner estuary) is c0.9m higher than at Southend (outer estuary), which is itself 1.6m below the corresponding level at London Bridge (PLA 1983, 41). The first-century data seems broadly compatible with the inner estuary curve, although it must be stressed that the latter is dated by radio carbon determinations, and cannot therefore be plotted accurately. The fourteenth-century data does not match so well, perhaps suggesting that either it (Milne and Milne 1982, fig. 43) or the curve (Devoy 1979) need modification at that point.

Given that the first-century London data seems to be consistent with the broadly contemporary evidence from the inner and outer estuary, it is

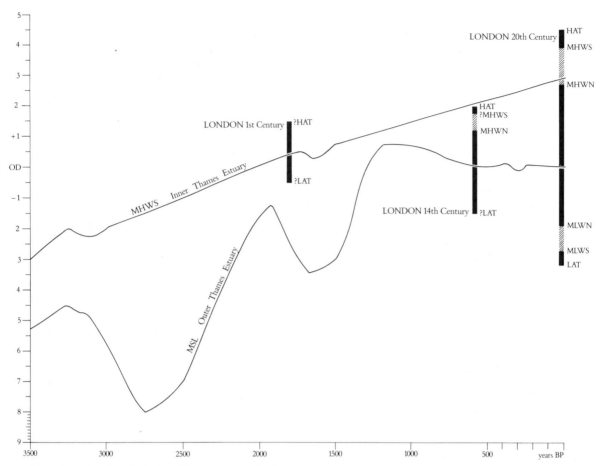

50 *The changing level of the Thames over the last 3500 years. Curves for inner estuary at Tilbury (Devoy 1979) and outer estuary near Foulness (Greensmith and Tucker 1973) plotted with levels of River Thames in London in first century, fourteenth century (Milne and Milne 1982) and twentieth century* AD *(PLA 1983). L or HAT = Lowest or Highest Astronomical Tide; MLWS or N = Mean Low Water Spring or Neap tide; MHWS or N = Mean High Water Spring or Neap tide; MSL = Mean Sea Level.*

possible to argue that the late or post-Roman regression clearly reflected in both those curves may also have been experienced in the City reach of the river. An analysis of mollusca (snails) from Roman foreshore deposits at Westminster, just 3km upstream of the Roman harbour, revealed that only one species shows any tolerance of brackish conditions but it is part of an otherwise entirely non-brackish fauna (Evans, in Limbrey and Greig, forthcoming). It is therefore possible that the tidal head lay east of Westminster throughout the Roman period. If this could be established unequivocally, it would be of considerable significance, as even the slightest decrease in river level at London itself would result in the tidal head moving eastwards, ie downstream away from the City. Associated changes in the width, salinity and tidal amplitude of the river would have materially altered the shape, form and vegetation cover of the banks. The river itself may well have begun cutting a deeper channel for itself, and may have begun scouring the former foreshore rather than gradually building it up as it did in the earlier tidal period. An eroded horizon was in fact identified at the Custom House site (Tatton-Brown 1974, 128) and on the late Roman levels at the St Magnus House site where it is suggested that river action probably caused disturbance of the remaining quay front and its infill (Miller *et al* forthcoming).

85

Perhaps the most important consequence for the history of the port of London would be that such a change in the tidal head would have affected navigation on the river, since boats could no longer be swept right up to the City on an incoming tide. Further research is now urgently required to establish the precise nature of the river in the late Roman period. What is certain is that the Thames subsequently began to rise and early to mid-Saxon radiocarbon dates were obtained from wood within clay deposited by the river at Westminster during this period (Mills 1980, 22). There seems little doubt that by the mid- to late-Saxon period London was sitting on a tidal reach of the Thames, ready to take advantage of the commercial potential such a situation offered.

CHAPTER 8

THE RIVER AS A RESOURCE

Today it is difficult to appreciate the overriding importance of the river to the population of Roman London. As a 200km long highway across southern Britain it was unrivalled, and for the citizens of London it was not only a major means of communication but was also an essential source of water for them and their livestock. In addition, its waters contained fish in abundance and it is this aspect which will be considered here. Although evidence from the recent waterfront excavations has thrown little light on the common occupation of fishing in the city reach, it has shown that such activities were practised in the mouth of the estuary and that London played an important role in this industry as both a market and a processing centre.

The sauce of the Thames

Some 12m to the north of the warehouses, remarkable evidence for the processing of fish by-products was found in an area between two domestic or possibly official buildings (Figs. 14d, 17a, 52; Bateman and Locker 1982). A small trench on the Peninsular House site exposed a sequence of east-west aligned timber drains representing continuous activity from the mid-first to the early fourth century. The alignment of these drains was square to a rectangular timber tank found some 5m to the east and arguably part of the same complex. Only the south-east corner of the tank was exposed, and it comprised a vertical post into the sides of which horizontally set planks were tenoned (Fig. 53). The structure was set 0.75m below the contemporary ground surface and close to the spring-line. However, it did not serve as a well since the thick clay packed around and beneath it shows that it was constructed to contain rather than to collect liquid. Dendrochronological analysis of the samples from the timbers suggest that the structure had been built in the first century. How long this tank remained in use is uncertain since it was truncated by modern basements. However, the drain sequence survived in better condition. One of the later timber-lined channels overlay a coin of Tacitus cAD 275 and both the channel and the contemporary timber floor to its north seem to have been enclosed within a lean-to building. Lying in this drain and spread out over the timber floor was a smashed amphora surrounded by thousands of tiny fish bones.

At first it was thought that the fish bone layer represented an unfortunate accident with an amphora of *garum*, the strong fish sauce manufactured on a large scale in several coastal towns in France and Spain. However subsequent analysis of the London deposit by Alison Locker of the Ancient Monuments Laboratory showed that the bones probably represented a local British catch rather than a foreign import (Locker 1983).

The work involved to reach this important conclusion was considerable. First, 2.5kg of the deposit were sieved, using a mesh of 250 microns and producing a residue of 650g composed entirely of small fish bones. Since this enormous quantity made total identification impractical, only sub-samples of set weight (5g, 10g and 20g) were analysed. The species represented were mainly herring (which does not occur south of the Bay of Biscay) and sprat, forming 84 per cent and 16 per cent respectively of the sample, although individual specimens of bass, flatfish and sandeel were also present. None of the herring was very large, suggesting that they had all been relatively young fish, and all parts of the skeleton were represented, indicating the presence of whole fish. All these species in their immature state could and still can be found in the Thames estuary, the composition of such a catch being very similar to what is now known as 'whitebait' (Wheeler 1978, 67 and Wheeler 1979, 70).

Together, the presence of the fish bone deposit and the nature of the structural evidence with which it was associated seem to suggest a building in which fish were processed. This may well have been for the production of a local variant of the popular fish sauce *garum*. Classical authors describe many different recipes for the making of

51 *First-century fishing by line and hand net: note Mediterranean harbour buildings in background. Scene shown on an oil lamp, c85mm diameter, reproduced here by kind permission of the British Museum.*

garum according to the fish available and the scale of the operation. For instance Pliny provides recipes for its manufacture based on small red mullet, sprats, anchovies, horse mackerel or mackerel making a mixture of them all; the best *garum* called *haimation* was made from the entrails of tunny fish and its gills, juice and blood. Pliny also describes how the sauce could be produced at a 'home brew' level. 'Put the fish into the brine in a new earthenware pot . . . put it on a good fire until it boils – ie until it begins to reduce' (Flower and Rosenbaum 1980, 22). The end of the manufacturing process was that the liquid was strained off as *garum* or *liquamen* and the solid residue sold off as

hallec. As Pliny points out, *hallec* was also specifically made – ie it was not simply a by-product – 'from very small fish that were otherwise useless' (Flower and Rosenbaum 1980, 23). So some fish sauces came with the bones and some – presumably the more upmarket products – were subsequently strained off. Whether the bones in the drain represent an accident with a jar of local *hallec* or with a jar of *garum* substitute before it had been strained off is impossible to say.

Along the south coast of Spain, the western seaboard of Morocco and the coast of Brittany the manufacture of *garum* and related fish products was undertaken on an extensive scale involving the

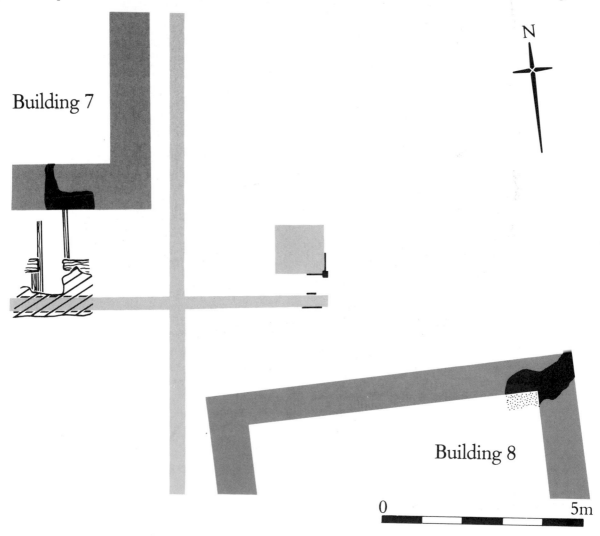

52 *A Romano–British fish processing plant. Plan showing remains of a timber floor, drain near Building 7 and water-retaining tank (Fig. 53) recorded on the Peninsular House site near* Pudding Lane. A broken amphora and a deposit of fish bones (shown hatched) covers the floor and drain.

89

53 *South-east corner of clay-packed timber tank (see Fig. 52). Note how planks join corner post.*

use of large rectangular lined tanks for fermentation and salting (Ponsich and Tarradell 1965 and Sanquer and Galliou 1972, 199–223). In London it is possible that the timber tank found to the east of the drain sequence was used similarly in the manufacture of this British fish sauce.

Fig. 17b shows that the proposed fish processing area lay not far from the early third-century waterfront and was therefore well situated to handle fish unloaded at the quays. It was only 12m to the north of the warehouses where *garum* amphoras were probably stored in quantity in the first and early second centuries (see Chapter 6).

Of all the amphoras found in London, some 20 per cent are associated with the Spanish *garum* trade, demonstrating that the traffic in this imported commodity was relatively important. A recent excavation in Southwark unearthed one such vessel complete with part of its original contents, the heads of Spanish mackerel (information from I. Tyers). It is ironic that the vessel smashed in the third-century drain was a Spanish amphora originally used to bring foreign *garum* into Britain and was probably over 100 years old when broken. The pot, long since emptied of its original contents, must have been re-used to store a local catch. Since there is little evidence for the continued importation of *garum* in the third century it was suggested that the Peninsular House deposit represented more evidence for the decline of imported luxury goods and of their replacement by local commodities (Bateman and Locker 1982, 207). On the other hand, the drain sequence and the tank feature were established in the first century, implying that local fish processing had begun even while foreign fish products were still being imported.

In the nineteenth century, whitebait fishing in the Thames required only a small net cast from small boats moored in the tideway (Wheeler 1979, 71). The ceramic lamp in Fig. 51 shows a representation of a similar operation in the harbour of Alexandria on the north African coast some 1800 years earlier. In this scene, a man casts a small hand held net while a second man fishes by line from a boat. Colonnaded warehouses of the port, possibly somewhat similar to the first-century warehouses described in Chapter 6, form the background to the picture. It seems that Roman fishing was mostly confined to coastal or inland waters and only involved relatively small boats such as these. Writing at the beginning of the third century,

Aelian, in *On the Characteristics of Animals*, describes the four kinds of fishing known to him: 'with nets, with a pole, with a weel, and with a hook' (Schofield 1959, 65).

His descriptions of fishing with nets and with a weel (a kind of trap) are particularly relevant for archaeologists since so little surviving material evidence for this important activity has been identified:

> Netting fish brings wealth . . . it requires a variety of gear, for instance rope, fishing line white and black, cord made from galingale, corks, lead, pine timber, thongs, *sumach*, a stone, papyrus, horns, a six oared ship, a windlass with handles, a *cottane*, a drum, iron, timber and pitch.
> . . . Fishing with a weel is a pursuit that calls for much craft and deep design and seems highly unbecoming to free men. The essentials are club-rushes unsoaked, withies, a large stone, anchors, sea weed, leaves of rushes and cypress, corks, pieces of wood, a bait and a small skiff (Schofield 1959, 65–67).

These comments suggest a level of technology and an industrial organisation far removed from the deep sea trawlers and factory ships of the present day. Whatever the scale of the operation represented by the deposit of fish bones described in this chapter, it still remains the earliest evidence yet found for a local fishing industry based in London.

Oyster culture

Fish was not the only marine resource exploited by the Romans. The writings of Pliny the Elder, Juvenal and others show that they were great connoisseurs of oysters. They knew what qualities to look for in a good oyster, and could identify oysters from different places by variations in taste and appearance. Montanus describes a man who, like Juvenal's gourmet, '. . . whether Circe's rock his oyster bore, or Lucerne Lake, or distant Richborough shore, knew at first taste' (Philpots 1890, 282).

The earliest of the many surviving references in ancient literature to the oysters of Roman Britain dates from c50 BC, shortly after Julius Caesar's expeditions (Philpots 1890, 40). However, Roman gourmets only became aware of British oysters during the administration of Agricola (AD 78–85), when Agrippa is said to have imported them to

Rome (Philpots 1890, 45). Later Macrobius tells how the Roman pontiffs of the fourth century AD always had oysters from *Rutupiae* (Richborough) at table, no doubt emulating Constantine the Great who returned from Britain with a decided liking for them.

Although oysters are marine creatures, they also form extensive colonies in estuaries and tidal inlets because river waters high in minerals leached from the land surface promote the growth of the micro organisms upon which they feed. The main Richborough oyster beds must have lain in Sandwich Bay but beds occurred around the north Kent and Essex coasts extending into the mouth of the Thames.

These natural resources were extensively exploited by the Romans, but it has been suggested that they introduced oyster culture to Britain (Philpots 1890, 254), with the formation of artificial oyster beds similar to those previously developed in Italy (Fig. 54).

During the excavations at Pudding Lane, two large deposits of oyster shells were found, and the analysis of samples from them has thrown light on the Romano-British oyster industry. The earliest group was found beneath the late first-century landing stage, and formed part of a massive dump or midden over 1m deep which had accumulated while the open-work landing stage was operational (Fig. 14b). They exhibited a large range of sizes and were not particularly regular in shape; some were deformed, attached in groups or had shell debris. It seems likely that the oysters came from a natural population that had not been worked but some selection with regard to size had taken place during collection. The shells were mostly younger than would be considered optimum for consumption today.

The conditions of burial of the shells allowed the preservation of parts of the dark brown or black horny scales on the right valves and in some instances the ligament or hinge which joins the two valves of the shell in life. However, a very high proportion of the shells were badly broken, suggesting that they were opened in a most inept way.

The organisms which have infested or encrusted the oyster shell during life give a clue to the place where the oyster was bred. The most common infestation in the shells from under the landing stage was caused by a small worm called *Polydora ciliata* although the degree of infestation was slight. These worms are characteristic of hard sandy or clay grounds, particularly in warm, shallow water. These conditions prevail in the Thames estuary itself and around the Essex and north Kent coasts. Bearing in mind that the sea level in the first century AD was 3–4m lower than at the present time, the minimum salinity required by oysters (a range of 28–36 parts per 1000, c3 per cent) would not have been found as far upstream as Roman London. The oysters from the waterfront excavation were not therefore grown very close to the City, but, it seems reasonable to suggest, may have been collected from lower down the Thames estuary, possibly from the same beds as the Rutupian oysters.

That the oysters were clearly opened on the spot and the shells dumped in such quantity under and around the landing stage poses a problem. It is possible that the oysters were eaten by crew members of the coastal barges transporting them, or that they were sold direct to eager customers from the moored boats as was done at Victorian Billingsgate. A third possibility is that the midden represents the residue of a process in which the meat was systematically removed from the shells to be preserved for later consumption.

To be enjoyed at their best, oysters should be eaten alive, which necessitates their rapid transfer from sea bed to consumer. However, because of the difficulties and expense involved in transportation, at least some of those oysters destined for inland markets may have been pickled, a process certainly practised in the seventeenth century. Since most of the fish eaten by the common people in Roman times would have been salted, it is reasonable to suppose that some oysters were similarly preserved. That salt pans in existence before the Roman invasion were sometimes constructed alongside natural populations of oysters – as at Paglesham in Essex for example, where those same pans are now used as storage pits for oysters – could be argued to lend support to this suggestion, although the coincidence may simply reflect the intertidal habitat required by both industries. It has also been suggested (Flower 1958) that washing oysters with vinegar and storing them in a pitch-coated receptacle would have prevented the decay of encrusting or infesting organism on the shells, but may not have materially affected the survival rate of the oysters. An *olla* or wide-necked coarse-ware jar covered inside and out with bitumen is recorded from an early Roman pit at Richborough, where a contemporary cellar believed to have been used for cool storage of wine and oysters was also found.

The first-century oyster shells found on the London waterfront during the Pudding Lane excavations were therefore probably harvested from natural oyster beds on the north Kent coast. A second group of oyster shells found at Pudding Lane, this time incorporated in the foundations of second-century buildings, exhibited noticeably different characteristics from the earlier one. As before, preservation was good. The shells, however, were larger and rounder, the right valves thin and flat. There was little distortion although a few pairs were stuck together. The majority of the left valves had deep cups indicating the short, thick meat so desirable in a good oyster. The inside of the shells often showed the pure white, unblemished surface said to be typical of the Whitstable oyster. The heels of the left valves were attached to oyster, mussel and cockle cultch. Cultch is material laid down for the oyster larvae or spat to settle on during the spawning season. This all suggests that a deliberate attempt had been made to catch spat from an already breeding population (probably natural). The cut marks on the shells were clearly defined and the breakage pattern much less and usually restricted to a certain area of the shell margin showing an increased dexterity with opening.

Many of the features recorded point to some sort of cultivation to improve the number and quality of the oysters. This supports the contention of various modern writers that the Romans introduced oyster culture to Britain. It seems unlikely that the elaborate form of oyster culture such as that practised in Italy (Brothwell and Brothwell 1969; Coste 1861; Gunther 1897) would have been necessary in Britain where there must have been many unworked natural beds around the coasts. If the beds around the Thames estuary and the Kent and Essex shores were inadequate to meet the increasing demands made upon them (which analysis of the second-century shell sample from London suggests may have been the case), they could have been enlarged and improved quite simply. Since the bedrock on the foreshore was much firmer here, artificial beds could be easily created by taking young oysters from the natural beds and relaying them in new, adjacent areas. Spat collection would have been enhanced by laying down old oyster, mussel or cockle shells close to a breeding population. Dredging would help re-

move any silt accumulations, plants or pests. Separating the young brood-oysters before three years would prevent distortion, allowing each individual to mature into the desired shape.

OYSTER TRANSPORTATION

By what method or route fresh British oysters would have travelled to Rome and how they survived is a matter for speculation, although oysters can survive for up to ten days out of water. To keep the two valves firmly shut in order to retain the little reservoir of fluid around the meat, the shells must be tightly packed together, cupped valve lowermost. Baskets, barrels, bags and possibly jars may have been used in Roman times. The condition of oysters will ultimately deteriorate no matter how well packed, so the time taken to transport them would therefore have been crucial. Oysters sent to London by river or by the long sea route to Italy could have been laid loose in the boat and continually doused with refreshing sea water, a relatively cheap method of transportation.

EATING OYSTERS

Although the Romans extolled the delights of eating oysters and the subtleties of their flavour, they also had a well documented aversion to eating anything in its natural state, and even raw oysters were served with spicy sauces like *garum* or *liquamen* (see above). One example of a sauce especially made to accompany oysters and other shellfish combined pepper, bay leaf, malabathrum, plenty of cumin, honey, vinegar and liquamen. Raw oysters were frequently eaten as part of the *gustatio* (hors d'oeuvres) at the *cena* (evening meal). The short bladed knives commonly found on Roman sites, would be ideal for opening shells. There was a special little spoon called a *cocleare* used for eating eggs and shellfish. It had a pointed handle convenient for picking snails and other molluscs from their shells.

Marine molluscs would be used in cooked dishes. A simple dish which was probably served cold was *Embractum Baianum*: minced oysters, mussels, sea urchins, chopped toasted pine kernels, rue, celery, corriander, cumin, passum (sweetened cooking wine), liquamen, Jerico date and oil were placed in a saucepan and cooked. The finished article may have been served on a dish called a *conchiclar*, a shell shaped dish like the bronze scallop shaped dishes at Pompeii. Pliny mentions that oysters were frequently eaten with a special type of bread but gives no details. Some of the

cooked dishes were most elaborate. One, called a 'patina with milk', incorporated twenty-six ingredients, including boiled brains, Leucanian sausages, chicken, jellyfish, oysters and cheese, all arranged in layers in a dish with a sauce poured over it and garnished with fresh sea urchins.

OTHER USES

It is interesting to note that oysters were not only delicious to eat but were believed to possess many other useful properties. Pliny records that oysters could be used as a mild laxative or, boiled in their shells, were efficacious for streaming colds. Calcined oyster shells relieved sore throats and treated abscesses when mixed with honey. When mixed with water, they were applied to ulcerations of the head, and were used to improve the complexion of ladies. The ashes were also sprinkled on burns, used as tooth powder, or when mixed with figs and pitch, could plug leaks in baths. Finally, whipped raw oysters were thought to cure chilblains.

The Romans certainly exploited British natural oyster beds and, if the analysis of the London material is correct, may even have introduced oyster culture to the Province. This would have helped the demands of an expanding market which not only saw oysters from the south east coast sent in bulk to London and its immediate hinterland, but also as far south as Rome itself. However, the Romans stationed in the Empire's most northerly province may have been hard pressed to decide whether to savour the oysters as food, or use them to cure the colds and chilblains from which they no doubt suffered.

54 *The distorted shape of oysters grown naturally in crowded beds (top) contrasted with examples cultivated artificially in less cramped conditions (bottom).*

CHAPTER 9
SHIPS AND BARGES

The Elizabethan harbour of London must have been crowded with river traffic for, quite apart from the 'great ships and other vessels of burthen', the contemporary historian John Stow observed that there were some 2000 wherries and other small boats working on this reach of the river (Stow 1970, 13). Although the boat nomenclature is sometimes rather obscure, it seems that there were three main classes of vessel on the medieval London Thames: sea-going ships (*nave*), barges (*shoute*) and the smaller boats (*batteli*). The relative sizes of such craft can be appreciated from the discovery of wrecks such as the barges found in 1971 near Trig Lane (Marsden 1979) and from various contemporary illustrations, and may be deduced from the tolls charged at Billingsgate which, as early as cAD 1000 were a halfpenny for a small boat, one penny for a larger ship with sails, and four pence for a merchantman. How this picture compares with the traffic in the Roman harbour is less certain as there is little documentary or pictorial evidence for Roman shipping in London. Nevertheless an assessment of this crucial aspect of the harbour study has been attempted based primarily on the wrecks which have been found near the City, a knowledge of the contemporary tidal conditions, and comparison with the types of craft known to have been used on the River Tiber between Ostia and Rome and on the River Rhine. This chapter will not examine the construction details, techniques or traditions of Roman shipbuilding, since this absorbing subject has been considered elsewhere (eg Marsden 1977), but concentrates on the use of different classes of vessel on the Roman River Thames and the handling of the cargoes they carried. First, the Mediterranean system will be considered and contrasted with that in northern Europe, after which the evidence for the London pattern will be suggested, and shown to owe something to both models.

Shipping on the Tiber and the Rhine

Before the great harbourworks were built at the mouth of the Tiber near Ostia in the mid-first century, some merchantmen could be rowed upriver to Rome while other shallow-draft vessels were towed by teams of men trudging along a towpath (Casson 1965, 32). But the standard size of merchantmen was approximately 340 tons, and these larger vessels had to anchor offshore in the open sea and transfer their cargoes to shallow draft lighters, probably known as *lenunculi auxiliarii*. Alternatively, they sailed to the well-protected harbour at Puzzoli (*Puteoli*) where their cargoes could be loaded onto coastal vessels small enough to negotiate the Tiber. Once the ambitious artificial harbour project was completed (Fig. 4) the merchantmen could be berthed against the deep-water quays in relative safety, and their cargoes could be manhandled into the neighbouring warehouses or onto the special boats designed to be towed up the Tiber to Rome. These were known as *naves codicariae*, and have been identified with vessels depicted on surviving reliefs and frescoes (Casson 1965, 36). They had rounded hulls, a readily-identifiable stem and prow and a mast placed towards the front of the vessel. Since this was usually shown without a yard or sail, it could have been used for attaching to a tow line. However, it has also been suggested that these common craft could be fitted with a spritsail, and thus could travel under their own power when required. As such, they were as suited for coastal work as for the long haul up the Tiber to Rome.

Different types of vessel are associated with the rivers of northern Europe such as the Rhine. The pictorial evidence for them has been discussed in a paper by Dr Ellmers (1978) but it is the results of the excavations of wrecks of a particular type of barge on such sites as Zwammerdam in the Netherlands (de Weerd 1978) and Pommeroeul in Belgium (de Boe 1978) which will be considered here (Fig. 57). The vessels in question were flat-bottomed barges up to 34m long. They were constructed by hollowing out a tree trunk into a standard dugout form, splitting it down the middle

55 *Sea-going merchantmen of a similar type to the County Hall ship with a barge or lighter alongside.*

longitudinally and inserting planks between the two halves to form the floor. Both halves of the original dugout trunk thus became strong watertight members joining the floor to the sides. The structure could then be strengthened with ribs and its sides heightened by adding a run of planking. The mast, which was set towards the front of the vessel, was large enough to support a sail in some examples but in others was only used for towing.

Barges of this type must have been among the most common working boats on the inland waterways of northern Europe although their shallow draft and keel-less profile meant that they were not suitable for service on the North Sea. The produce they carried must therefore have been transferred to or from round-hulled seagoing ships

in harbours situated on estuaries. There is considerable evidence for such transhipment sites in northern Europe. Two of these, Colijnsplaat and Domburg lying on the River Scheldt in the Netherlands, are of especial interest since they provide clear proof of contact with British traders (Hassall 1978). Both had shrines to the goddess Nehalennia, a 'guardian' or 'guiding' goddess, to whom altars had been erected by merchants to commemorate safe sea crossings. Careful study of the dedications on these altars has shown that pottery and perhaps wine destined for Britain and salt, fish and possibly woollen clothes imported from there were handled at these ports, presumably being transferred between ship and river barge at this point.

Roman wrecks in the Thames

Roman wrecks were found on the site of County Hall in 1910 (Fig. 56), in Bermondsey in 1958 and at Blackfriars in 1962. Careful study by Peter

Marsden suggests that three quite distinct classes of vessel are represented: respectively a modest sea-going merchantman, a flat-bottomed lighter which could only have operated on the river, and a small sailing ship designed for tidal coastal waters as well as inland waterways. The County Hall ship was round-hulled and may have been up to 20m long, 5m wide with a draft of less than 2m. It was built in the third century in a similar fashion to vessels known from the Mediterranean and may have been a small sea-going merchantman (Marsden 1974). Since the Roman Thames was tidal (Chapter 7) and since the ship could not be beached at low tide, this vessel would have had to anchor in mid-stream in the deep-water channel where its cargo could have been off-loaded onto lighters of the type excavated at New Guys House, Bermondsey (Fig. 55). That particular example was c16m long and over 4m wide, flat-bottomed, and therefore capable of sitting on the foreshore at low tide (Marsden 1965). The Blackfriars I ship was also flat-bottomed, some 16m long and c6m across, with a draft of under 2m (Fig. 59). Although it was an ideal craft for working the tidal river, it is clear that it must also have sailed round the coast, since its timbers were infested with marine wood-boring creatures (Marsden 1967). The second-century vessel recently found outside St Peter Port, Guernsey, may have been of a similar type (*Int. J. Naut. Archaeol. 13. 4* (1984), 34–6).

Although no barges of the Zwammerdam type have yet been found in Britain, it is possible that they were in use here since the basic techniques required to build them were certainly to hand. Log boats, or dugout canoes, are known in the Roman period in this country, and also appear in contexts from 1500 BC to AD 1500, with thirteen examples from or close to the Thames (McGrail 1977; McGrail and Switsur 1979). In addition, a second-century drain which disgorged through the Roman quay in London was built from a series of well-made dugout tree trunks laid end to end and carefully scarfed together (Fig. 58).

It seems clear that the tidal conditions in the Thames would have prevented the largest Roman merchantmen docking directly against the London quays, for the City was not a deep-water port. As has already been suggested, those which did penetrate that far upstream would have anchored in mid-stream and off-loaded onto lighters of the New Guys House type, the British equivalent of the *lenunculi auxiliarii*. Better situated harbours on the coast, such as Richborough or Dover, probably accommodated the principal sea-going vessels, at which point the goods would be transferred to vessels of the Blackfriars I type, able to make the run around the coast and up the river to London. Unlike the *naves codicariae* on the Tiber, these vessels would not require towing on the Thames, but could take advantage of the tides.

Handling the cargoes

Although the citizens of Roman London may not therefore have seen the largest ships of the day, they did see the merchandise that such vessels had once carried, after it had been transferred from river barge to ship on the northern European coast, offloaded at a British sea port, and manhandled aboard a smaller vessel for the next stage of its long voyage. This double or treble-handling of cargoes seems to be a feature of the Roman distributive system, and clearly required considerable manpower.

A particularly good illustration of the labour involved is provided by an assessment of the size of the storage jars favoured by the Romans. The Roman term *amphora* describes a measure approximating to one Roman cubic foot, or 48 *sextarii*, a *sextarius* being less than a pint. The equivalent modern measure is approximately 26 litres, or 6 gallons. Fairly standard amphora shapes were used for certain commodities, but the heights, girths and wall thicknesses differed. To determine the measure of a commodity being transported, the Romans weighed the amphora jar empty and then again when full, subtracted the weight of the jar, and wrote the result on it: standardisation of size was not therefore important. As a result, there was a considerable range in the capacity, and therefore also the weight, of the amphoras handled in Roman London. Most had a capacity of 24–30 litres, and would therefore have weighed some 50kg on average, but the capacity of some such as the Camulodunum 198 was only 3.5 litres, while the Dressel 20 types could carry from 45 to 80 litres of olive oil, which would weigh up to 100kg or more. For comparison, three Roman barrels found in London have estimated capacities of 400, 500 and 1000 litres (Wilmott 1982, 47): these containers would have been rolled, rather than carried. By contrast, amphoras are generally wide at the girth and tapered at both ends, so that they are well-balanced and convenient for carrying sideways or upright at shoulder height. Most have a knob or

56 *Roman shipwreck found near the Thames when County Hall was built in 1910, ready for transportation to the London Museum.*

spike at the base which acts as a third handle when the vessel is lifted or inverted for pouring, and some have a very small flat base serving the same function. A base big enough for the amphora to stand on would give no purchase for lifting.

The thousands of amphoras which could be transported in one shipload were sometimes all of one type, like the Dressel IB wine amphoras on the Madragne de Giens wreck, but more often comprised several different types. The method of stacking varied with the size and shape of both the ship and the cargo, but the amphoras would have always been well packaged to prevent breakages. In the Madragne de Giens wreck, amphoras were stacked in the ship's hull on their side in layers packed tightly with rushes and heather. By contrast a third-century bas relief from Trier depicts a small barge or lighter with amphoras stacked upright in baskets or rush containers.

Amphora loads were heavy: it has been estimated that the 3000 amphoras carried in the wrecked Grand Conglue ship weighed about 150 tons and those in the Madrange de Giens wreck about 300 to 350 tons. Since both vessels were also carrying other cargo the total tonnage would have been greater. Such heavy cargoes were by no means exceptional, for there are records of shipments on the large imperial grain carriers of over 1000 tons, all of which had to be manhandled on and off the ship.

How unloading would have been conducted in London would obviously depend on how the ships moored, and unfortunately this question has not as yet been satisfactorily resolved. There seems to have been minimal provision for ships to berth directly alongside the quay. Little evidence for mooring posts, rings or bollards has been found, although it must be stressed that the upper face of the uppermost members of the timber quay itself was very decayed and often disturbed by subsequent activity. In addition, the heads of the braces protruding south of the quay face would have been an impediment unless they were shielded. A system utilising small jetties such as that recorded on the western quay (Fig. 34) or mooring posts set well to the south of the quay, and therefore beyond the limit of excavation, is a possibility. The careful investigation of the contemporary foreshore which lies beneath Thames Street itself would help to resolve this problem. Fortunately, these deposits are not at present under threat of disturbance or destruction and a later generation of

archaeologists should be able to examine them if a future development results in their excavation.

In conclusion, it can be suggested that the Roman harbour in London, like its Elizabethan successor, was visited by a variety of ships, the loading and unloading of which would have required a supply of casual, or at least seasonal, labour since seagoing traffic would be less likely to operate in the winter months. The tidal Thames could have been a treacherous river for large vessels attempting to navigate between its shifting shoals and islands, as a comparison of Figs. 49b and 49c shows: a pilot or a local crew would certainly have been required to ensure a safe journey. The largest seagoing ships may therefore have concentrated on the run across the North Sea, collecting a cargo from the transhipment ports such as Domburg and discharging it at coastal ports such

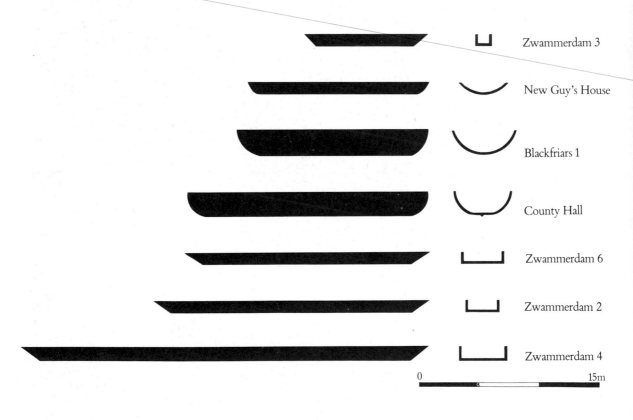

Zwammerdam 3

New Guy's House

Blackfriars 1

County Hall

Zwammerdam 6

Zwammerdam 2

Zwammerdam 4

0   15m

57 *The approximate size of Roman wrecks from the Thames compared with the Zwammerdam barges from the Rhine shown in elevation and cross-section.*

58 *This Roman drain was constructed from carefully hollowed-out tree trunks, a similar technique to that used to build the dugout barges found on the Rhine (0.5m scales).*

59 *Sailing ships of the Blackfriars I type lying on the London foreshore at low tide, with first-century waterfront warehouses in the background. Reconstruction by R. Embleton.*

as Dover. The latter must have been a major harbour, some of the installations of which have been recorded (Rigold 1969), since the fleet of the *Classis Britannica* had a base there (Philp 1981, 113–8). However, the harbours protected by the Isle of Thanet and the forts at Reculver and Richborough were perhaps more conveniently situated for the handling of shipments destined specifically for the City. In this respect, Roman London was perhaps more like Rome, serviced by barges, lighters and other small ships, rather than Ostia which handled the larger vessels. Although the volume of traffic passing through provincial London could not be expected to approach that of the Imperial capital, it was probably sufficient to provide employment for a fleet of versatile vessels of the Blackfriars I type.

CHAPTER 10
TRAFFIC AND TRADE

Introduction

By the late first century London had probably become the largest town in the province; just meeting its daily needs would have required a considerable movement of goods and produce, both by road and river. In addition, more exotic merchandise was brought in from all corners of the Empire, much of which would have passed over the quays in the harbour. For example, recent excavations have yielded a bracelet of ivory, presumably from north Africa, amber beads from the Baltic and fragments of two almost identical gold necklaces with emerald beads. The emeralds were mined in Austria or Egypt (E.A. Jobbins and R. Harding pers. comm.), and the gold probably came from Spain or South Wales, but since similar fine jewellery was worn by the upper classes throughout the Empire and styles tended to be copied by skilled local craftsmen, it is not known if the necklaces were imported complete or were assembled in London. In fact, just as in medieval and modern times, it is possible that London itself was a centre of jewellery-making. A gold-refiner's premises in the Cannon Street area has long been known (Marsden 1975, 100), and possible evidence of gem-cutting – perhaps by immigrant craftsmen – has recently been discovered at a site in Eastcheap, where a cache of one onyx and three nicolo intaglios has been found in a mid-first-century pit (Henig, forthcoming). The gems are magnificently cut and, but for the fact that one of them appears to be unfinished, would normally be thought to have been imported.

Although most immediately recognisable, these 'exotic' items probably formed only a tiny proportion of the total goods brought into Roman London. The scale and diversity of the importation of manufactured products, foodstuffs and raw materials can only be discerned through careful analysis of the finds from archaeological excavations. Building stone can usually be traced to a particular region, and sometimes even to an individual quarry, and by studying metalwork or glassware on sites both in Britain and abroad it is sometimes possible to identify the distant origins of distinctive vessel-types. Of all forms of evidence pottery is probably the best indicator of London's overseas contacts, although its importance in the ancient economy can be overestimated. Its cheapness and fragility, and the uselessness and durability of broken sherds have combined to ensure that a greater proportion of the pottery used in antiquity has survived to the present day than of any other material. Over the years the detailed study of forms and fabrics, coupled with the excavation of kilns and the petrological analysis of clay, has meant that it is now possible to identify the source of at least 70 per cent of the vessels from London. It is a fortunate bonus that the large ceramic amphoras and certain other vessels were imported simply as containers. When study of the residues on their inner surfaces is combined with that of the source of the clays and of the painted inscriptions on their sides (Fig. 63), it sometimes becomes possible to chart the traffic of imported food and drink, items which are often unrepresented in the archaeological record.

Detailed descriptions of imported artefacts are included in the site archive reports which are housed in the Museum of London library. The present chapter summarises much of that work with the intention of investigating four distinct but related themes:

(i)   the scale and scope of the import traffic into Roman London;
(ii) the relationship between overseas and native suppliers;
(iii) the nature of the 'market';
(iv) the changing pattern of London's contacts with the rest of the Empire.

The study covers a very wide range of commodities, although particularly in respect of perishable goods such evidence as we have can only be the tip of the iceberg. First, consideration is given to building materials, the handling of which would

60 *The waterfront market in London where amphoras of imported products such as fish sauce or wine may have been sold.*

have been one of the more labour-intensive activities in the harbour. Then the changing emphasis in London's overseas contacts is first revealed in the evidence for imported food and drink. A similar pattern may be discerned in the importation of pottery, but here a further factor is introduced: the presence of local kilns which also supplied material for the London market. After a brief survey of the textile industry, radical changes in the range of imported products in the late Roman period are implied by the history of three more manufacturing industries, those producing lamps, glassware and figurines. Finally, all four themes are discussed together and tentative conclusions drawn about the traffic that visited the Roman harbour.

Building materials from Britain and overseas

The builders of Roman London chose materials in widespread use in the cities of the Classical world, exploiting them in ways unseen in Britain before the invasion (Fig. 61). Tiles formed an important component of this 'new look' and they were supplemented in the first century by cheaper and less durable unfired bricks. Local brickearth was used for the latter while tiles were mostly made from London Clay dug outside the immediate locality of the town and on the Thames foreshore at low tide (Fig. 14a). The supply of both posed no transport difficulties but the rapid rate of building, particularly in the late 60s and 70s, meant that additional tiles had to be obtained from other districts. Some, made from a yellow-buff coloured clay, are likely to have come from Kent since a kiln producing tiles of this type has been recorded at

61 *A considerable proportion of Roman London's imports would have been the brick, stone, tile and timber needed for the building trades.*

Eccles (Detsicas 1967, 170), but they ceased to be used in London after the mid-second century. Even as late as the fourth century a small proportion of tiles was still being obtained from kilns sited at least 50 miles from the town, but by now the centres of supply seem to have shifted northwards. The most recognisable type, roof and box-tiles in a distinctive soft, soapy fabric with shell inclusions, came from the Bedfordshire–Northamptonshire area.

London possessed no local stone suitable for masonry work. Essential supplies, therefore, had to be quarried elsewhere and its use was kept to a minimum except for purposes of ostentation where expense was no object. For foundations and coursing of load-bearing walls chalk, flint and Kentish Rag, a durable grey-coloured sandy limestone from the Hythe Beds of the Weald, were used. A small amount of Horsham stone and Pennant Grit was also imported, probably mainly for roofing. Such stones were principally transported by water to London. This is illustrated by the wreck of the Blackfriars barge, discovered in 1962, which sank in the Thames in the second century while still carrying its cargo of Ragstone (Marsden 1967, 39). As none of these stones lent themselves to ornamentation the Romans turned to Lincolnshire Limestone, particularly that quarried at Barnack in Northamptonshire, which involved transporting it for a considerable distance. Consequently, it was chiefly restricted to public works, such as the monumental arch, where expense was of less significance than political prestige (Blagg 1980). Some blocks, nevertheless, appear to have found their way into private use and were carved into tombstones, sarcophagi and column bases, such as the ones found on the Pudding Lane and Regis House sites.

Marble was another expensive commodity but it was a fairly common sight in London (Pl. 6a), particularly once the town grew in administrative importance towards the end of the first century. There is no archaeological evidence to suggest that continental marble was imported into London for building work before cAD 70 (Pritchard, forthcoming). However, Purbeck marble, a fossiliferous limestone which takes a high polish, was certainly in use in London before this date. Its initial exploitation by the Romans may have followed from their military campaigns in the South West, which took the army close to where the stone outcrops in Dorset (Beavis 1970, 194). Good communications by road as well as by sea assisted the rapid spread in its use throughout southern Britain, and in this respect London followed rather than set the fashion. Other British stones, especially a grey, calcareous shale from the Weald and fine-grained white limestone from both the southern chalklands and the belt of lias in Somerset, were also quarried and transported to London by the third quarter of the first century. These stones were worked into square or triangular elements and laid down in geometrical patterns to form paving. *Opus sectile* paving was much less common, however, than the contemporary black-and-white floor mosaics made from much smaller chips of the same type of stones. Although small cubes of white Carrara marble were also occasionally incorporated into floor mosaics during the late first century, this use of marble was rare in London. In the second and third centuries the increased vogue for multi-coloured pavements was met simply by using broken fragments of tile possessing a wide range of colour tones, in addition to white and grey-hued stones. An example of this was to be seen in the second-century bath in Building 6 (Pl. 5b).

By contrast, to create patterned wall-inlays coloured as well as white marbles were used and those shipped to London included purple veined *pavonazzetto* from Phrygia, white and green banded *cipollino* from Euboea and polychrome *semesanto* from Skyros (Pl. 6a). Other stones were porphyry (both red and green), black carboniferous limestone and various diorites. A few of these stones were obtained from quarries in the eastern desert of Egypt, which were increasingly exploited during the first century AD, but they need not have been shipped directly to Britain and could have been transported via Rome, where a large quantity of surplus marble was stockpiled over many years (Ward-Perkins 1980, 26). London's trade with South Gaul also included green *campan vert* and black and white marble from the Pyrenees. The wide variety of coloured stones available in London is clearly illustrated by a late third-century dump in the south-western quarter of the city. It was found close to the waterfront near St Peter's Hill (Williams 1983), and comprised veneers cut from nineteen different types of decorative stone. The importation of foreign marble into London continued until at least the early fourth century. A dedication from the ruins of the Temple of Mithras carved in a coarse-grained white marble, possibly from Thasos has been dated on the basis of its inscription to AD 307–8 (*RIB* 4). However, the overall expense meant that demand for marble was probably always restricted to a wealthy minority, who had access to supply networks and to whom the normal patterns of trade did not apply.

The demand for exotic material, perhaps quarried many hundreds of miles away, could therefore be met when the resources and patronage were available. However, the bulk of the building material required for Roman London – timber, tiles, daub and sand – was obtained within a small radius of the town. This pattern would have been reflected in the supply of most other raw materials brought into the city but for which no archaeological evidence is preserved. As such, it highlights the role of the new town as a major consumer market and shows that merely meeting its everyday needs would have had a considerable impact on its immediate environment.

Imported food and drink

Although milk products, meat, poultry, fresh fruit and vegetables were presumably produced locally, less perishable commodities such as olive oil, grain, wine, salt and preserved fish and fruit products were transported over long distances in the Roman period. The main commodities imported into Britain were Mediterranean foodstuffs and wine from France, Spain and Italy, North Africa and the

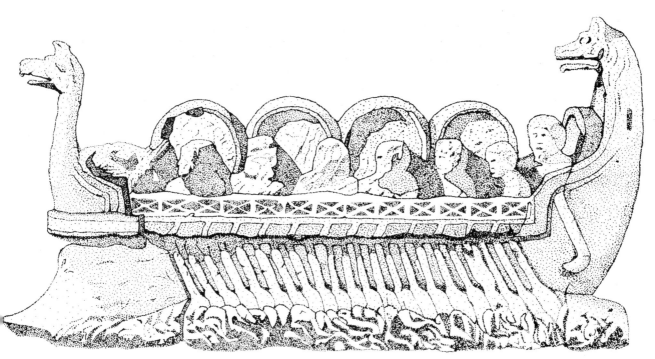

62 *Large Roman wine barrels transported by sea shown on a tombstone from Neumagen in the Rheinisches Landesmuseum, Trier.*

East Mediterranean. These were carried in large sealed ceramic amphoras, sherds of which are often found on excavations, but were presumably also transported in sacks, barrels, baskets, leather skins and other containers for which there is considerably less archaeological evidence. Locally produced commodities are also thought to have been brought into London in ceramic containers. Salt produced in large coastal salterns may have been transported in pitch-sealed shell-tempered jars, of which there are quantities in London. Honey, which was the only known Roman sweetener, is thought to have been transported in smaller lid-seated jars although no particular jar type has been identified.

An altar from Colijnsplaat, a Roman harbour in the Netherlands used by merchants sailing between Britain and the Rhineland, depicts a barge carrying barrels (Ellmers 1978, fig. 15; cf Fig. 62) and barrels and barrel staves have been found in quantity on Rhineland sites (Ulbert 1959). Thirteen have also been recorded reused in wells on first- and second-century waterlogged sites in London (Wilmott 1982, 23), and evidence for ten more (usually in the form of discarded staves) on the recent harbour excavations. The latest example recorded so far dates from the late third century, and was found just to the north of Building 2; but there is little other evidence for late Roman barrels in the City. V. Straker identified the wood used for the waterfront barrels, of which nine were cut from non-native softwoods. Seven were silver fir (*Abies alba*), which grows in the mountains of southern and central Europe, or cedar (*Cedrus libani*) from the Lebanon or Asia Minor. One was a larch (*Larix decidus*) or spruce (*Picea abies*) from a similar habitat as the silver fir; another was also a softwood but the exact species could not be identified, and the last example was oak (*Quercus sp.*) which is indigenous to Britain and much of continental Europe. Thus the identification of the species used for barrel manufacture has also established clear evidence of long-distance traffic, while the scarcity of barrels from late Roman contexts in London suggests that this traffic had declined markedly by the mid-third century. Wine may well have been a main commodity carried in this way, although epigraphic evidence shows that fish sauce and salt were also transported in barrels.

It was the study of amphora sherds from London sites which, however, provided the clearest evidence that Mediterranean commodities such as wine were imported as early as AD 50–60. A large

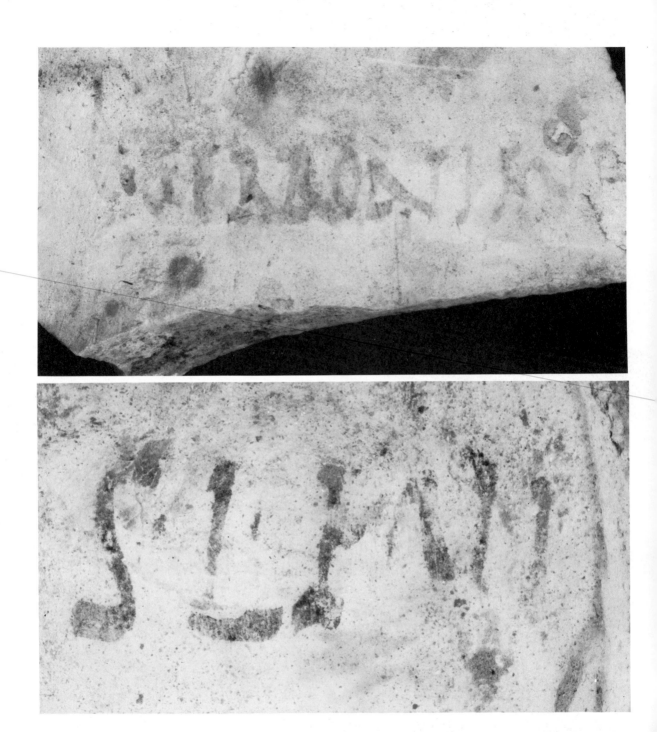

63 *The weight, contents, and name of the owner were often written on the body of amphoras and some examples from London excavations are shown here. MUR(ia) refers to brine or pickle; S.L.F.T. means uncertain; ACERRON(I) FUR means 'from the estate of Casius Acerronius Fur'.*

quantity of these early amphoras were used for wine from Southern (central) Italy, Southern France, the Greek island of Rhodes, Spain and other, as yet unidentified, sources. Southern Italy was one of the most renowned areas of Roman viticulture producing *crus* like the famous Falernian wine of Campania (Callendar 1965, 46–7; Sealey and Davies forthcoming). Southern France, principally the province of Gallia Narbonnensis, also produced and exported large quantities of wine. Rhodian wine is known to have been fairly good and inexpensive and may have been supplied primarily as a *vin ordinaire* for the army. One variety in particular, *passum*, a sweet dessert wine, seems to have been very highly regarded in antiquity (Sealey forthcoming). All these wines came from well-established areas of viticulture which were either already major exporters, or were just beginning to expand their market when Britain became part of the Roman Empire.

Smaller quantities of sherds of olive-oil, grape-syrup (*defrutum*) and fish or fish-sauce amphoras are also found in early London contexts. Olive oil and its by-products were widely used in the Roman Empire for cooking and lighting, as well as for lubrication and sealing wood (Fig. 65; White 1982). The chief source of export to London in the first and second centuries was Southern Spain, especially the province of Baetica. Here oil was produced on imperial and private estates and 'bottled' in distinctive globular amphoras. It was then shipped up the east coast of Spain to the mouth of the Rhone from where it was transported further eastwards or northwards up the Rhône-Rhine or Rhône-Loire river routes (Peacock 1978). It is also possible that shipments may have been carried up the west coasts of Spain and France, although there is very little evidence for this. In this period, other products exported principally from Spain (although manufactured in many Mediterranean countries) include *defrutum* or *sapu*, a sweet grape syrup used to improve bitter or sub-standard wine and for various medicinal and culinary purposes (White 1982), and the strong

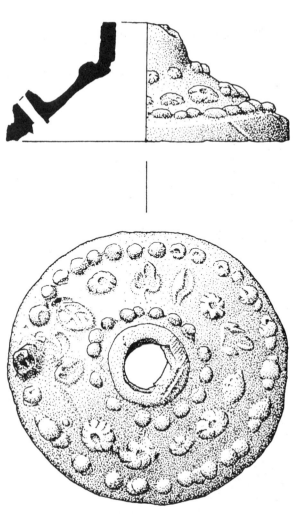

65 *Upper part of an unusual pottery vessel, c70mm in diameter, probably from France, found near Cannon Street, London in 1982. It was made in a mould and had a large filling hole and small pouring spout. Similar vessels found in Italy and North Africa are thought to have contained olive oil.*

64 *This amphora was found in the Thames estuary complete with its contents of 6000 olives. Photograph by kind permission of the National Maritime Museum, Greenwich.*

fish sauces such as *muria* (Fig. 63), *garum* and *liquamen*, which were made from fermented fish (see also Chapter 7). Sherds of an unprovenanced type of amphora which are found in some quantity in first-century deposits in London may have come from a more northerly Spanish province such as Tarraconensis. A complete example of this type recently recovered from the sea off the Kent coast was found to be still full of olives (Fig. 64). Figs and dates may have been imported in the small Eastern Mediterranean amphoras represented in early and later Roman deposits in London, but these amphoras never bear inscriptions and none have been found with their contents (Green 1980).

The peak of bulk commodity importation co-incided with London's expansion in the first and second centuries. Large quantities of amphora sherds were found in association with the late first and early second-century quays excavated on the Pudding Lane sites where they totalled over 70 per cent of the assemblages, as well as on sites away from the waterfront, such as those at Fenchurch Street and Lime Street. Most of these amphoras once contained oil, fish sauce or wine. 'Salt jars' are present in some quantity in this period and, unlike amphoras, are widely distributed with no particular concentration along the waterfront. A few sherds of briquetage containers used for brine evaporation have been found in London on an 'inland' site (Newgate Street) as well as on a waterfront site of this date, and two virtually complete briquetage containers of uncertain Roman date were recovered from the river bed in front of the early third-century quay at St Magnus House (Richardson, forthcoming). These large fragile containers may have been used for the transportation of salt but this was not common practice.

Sherds from Spanish amphoras are rare finds in mid- to late second-century deposits in London. There is no evidence for the fish and fruit product amphoras being imported after the end of the second century, or for oil amphoras after the mid-third century. It is possible that the Severan civil wars and subsequent Spanish land confiscations contributed to the diminution of trade between Spain and the rest of the Empire (Callendar 1965, 56) but it is also true that amphoras do not seem to have been used in the later Roman period as extensively as they were in the first and second centuries. That long distance trade, at least in the Mediterranean, may have declined after AD 200 is perhaps implied by the recording of a significantly smaller number of shipwrecks of this date (Hopkins 1980).

More localised exchange seems to have taken place between, for example, Britain and the Rhineland or Britain and the Netherlands, for which there is some early to mid-third-century epigraphic evidence (Hassall 1978). However, as whatever was carried was not transported in amphoras, there is no ceramic evidence to clarify the position. Wine was probably the major commodity to be exported from the Rhineland and Gaul to Britain. There is considerable archaeological or epigraphic evidence for Roman wine production in the Rhineland and Moselle in particular, and possible circumstantial evidence for production in the region of Bordeaux (Peacock 1978, 51). The small flat-bottomed amphoras found in London in third-century deposits at St Magnus House may have contained Gaulish wine, but they have only been recorded on this one site (Richardson, forthcoming). The export of amphora-borne wine from Southern Gaul to the North Western provinces seems to have stopped in the early-mid-third century, and other Gaulish wines and Rhenish wines may have been distributed in its place.

The small quantity of amphoras present on late third-century sites in London are nearly all North African and East Mediterranean, and are known to have contained olive oil and perhaps olives, dates, figs and other Eastern Mediterranean products. North African olive oil replaced Spanish oil in the third century, although for some time in the late second and early third century oil was coming into London from both sources (Green 1980). However, the North African product was not imported in anything like the quantity that Spanish oil had been, although there seems to have been a steady if diminished demand for oil in London until the early fifth century. The importation of products from North Africa and the East Mediterranean reflects a general trend towards contact with the Eastern Empire in the late Roman period, a trend which is underlined by the virtual cessation of imports of Western Mediterranean pottery to Britain after AD 250.

Pottery

Pottery in Roman times had much the same uses as it has today. Plates, dishes, bowls, cups, beakers and flagons were used at table, and flagons and cooking pots were used in the kitchen. The distinction between the two categories must often have been blurred, but it is reasonable to surmise that the thin-walled, coloured and often highly decorated pots (fine-wares) were used for eating and drinking and that the larger and coarser vessels (coarse-wares) were used for cooking and storage. Certain specialist vessel types like mortars (*mortaria*) were used for food preparation, and large container vessels (amphoras) were used for

66 *Imported and locally-made first- and second-century pottery commonly found in London (from left to right): jar from Highate Woods kilns; flagon from Brockley Hill; beaker from Cologne, Germany; mortar with lion-head spout from Lezoux, France. Drawn by D. Parfitt.*

transporting food and wine. The forms, styles and uses reflect their Mediterranean origin and the diet and lifestyle of the Roman people. The pottery used by the first inhabitants of the Roman settlement on the site of London came from a variety of sources. Much of it was made relatively locally, but a significant proportion was imported from elsewhere in the Roman world. Some types of pottery had been imported for almost a century before the conquest. Among the first imports in this period were fine red-slipped tablewares from Italy (Arretine ware) and Southern France (samian ware). Some of these forms were imitated by British potters, indicating a significant demand for these types from some sectors of the population in the years leading up to AD 43. It is against this background of importation and imitation that the developments in the mid- and later first century AD must be viewed.

FIRST CENTURY

Most of the coarser wares in use in early London came from relatively local sources. A substantial proportion were made in what might be termed the 'native' style – typologically and technologically very similar to pre-conquest products and un-doubtedly made by the successors of those who had been working in the south-east before AD 43. Some forms considered necessary for Roman cuisine were absent from this repertoire and these were supplied from other sources. Flagons, which rapidly become a significant part of the assemblage, seem to have been produced by potters conversant with Continental styles and techniques, many of whom were probably immigrants from Gaul or the Rhineland. One potter set up kilns very close to the new settlement of London, near the waterfront on the western side of the bridge and within the later city boundary. The style of his products suggests contact with western Switzerland or the Lyon area. The kilns do not seem to have operated for a long period but illustrate the wide potential range of influences bearing upon the developing Romano-British pottery industry during this formative period.

Many other producers supplied pottery to London during this early period, but the producers with kilns situated to the south of Verulamium were destined to become one of the largest flagon and mortarium manufacturers of the later first and early second century AD. Mortaria were another type of vessel considered necessary to the new culinary practices, although they seem to have been imported in very small quantities before the conquest. After the conquest demand boomed and was at first largely met by imports from a wide range of sources in Northern and Central Gaul, Italy and the Rhineland, but by cAD 70 most were of British manufacture. The Verulamium region potters, some of whom stamped their names on their work, supplied over 90 per cent of both the mortaria and flagons in use in London during the period AD 70–120.

The 'native' derived industries continued to produce pottery for the London market. The most successful during this same period was probably that based at Highgate Wood, less than 10km north of the city. The repertoire did not include flagons or mortaria, but concentrated on a range of bowls and jars. There was relatively little direct competition between the Highgate and Verulamium potters, and between them they supplied most of the coarse wares in use in London during the late first to early second century. Many of the smaller industries whose work is represented in mid-first-century deposits seem to have ceased production, or at least no longer supplied London, as the two principal producers increased their share of the market.

The demand for cups and plates in first- and second-century London was met almost entirely by imported samian, initially from southern Gaul, but later from central and east Gaul. The samian industry was one of the more remarkable economic phenomena of the ancient world. Although it is not possible to estimate the proportion of the output which was destined for export, the scale of production was vast, and the larger factories, such as that at La Graufesenque, supplied a high proportion of all the table wares in use in Britain, Gaul, the German provinces and parts of Italy during the mid and late first century AD. The internal organisation of the industry was complex. Graffiti recovered from excavations at the kiln sites list tasks performed by the various slaves and workmen employed by particular workshops. Tally lists scratched onto the bases of some pots indicate the large numbers of vessels in a single firing – as many as 30,000 in one instance. The vessels were made in a standard series of sizes and shapes, perhaps partly for ease of packing and transport.

Samian seems to have been considerably more common in London than on contemporary sites in the south-east. Almost a quarter of the pottery from some mid-first-century sites in the vicinity of the later Forum consists of samian ware. Hundreds of early second-century samian vessels stacked and sometimes burnt and fused together in a fire at what is thought to have been a waterfront warehouse on the Regis House site and hundreds more from the third-century waterfront at St Magnus House (Pl. 7a) indicate that samian was imported in considerable quantity. Compared with this, the other imported fine wares from Gaul, Italy and the Rhineland only occur in small quantities in the first century.

In contrast to the supply of plates and cups, most beakers in use in London during the first and early second centuries seem to have been made within the province, although often by potters who were clearly influenced by Continental styles. The exact location of these producers is not known, although some may have worked to the north of London, perhaps around Verulamium. By the early second century large numbers of barbotine decorated beakers of a type known as a 'poppy-head' beaker were being made for the London market by the Highgate Wood potters, who added this fine-ware form to their existing coarse-ware repertoire.

SECOND AND THIRD CENTURIES

The early to mid-second century was a period of radical change in the coarse-ware industry of south-east England. The principal stimulus was the development of a ware manufactured in Dorset in a purely 'native' style. Black Burnished ware (BB1) was produced in primitive bonfire kilns and was hand-made in a coarse fabric, but presented a well-made serviceable appearance. The main impact of BB1 in London was not in the proportion of the market that it took at this time, but rather in its effect on pre-existing producers such as Highgate. Within a few years, c60 per cent of all the Highgate jars in use in London seem to be derived from the BB1 type. These and imitation BB1, wheel-made grey BB2 jars, bowls and dishes were the dominant vessel types during the latter part of the second century. The Highgate industry probably ceased production towards the end of the century, superseded by producers based in Kent or Essex. By this date, a wider range of imported and locally-made beakers was available, and kilns in the Midlands or Colchester began producing mortaria for the northern market formerly supplied by the Verulamium region industry.

During the latter part of the second and early third centuries, imported fine-ware beakers may have become more common in London. The study of a large group of unused, imported pottery recovered from the infill of the Roman quay at St Magnus House gives a remarkable insight into the ceramic trade through London at this period. Samian forms the largest single group, but there are quantities of the fine black beakers which were produced at the same production centres in Central and East Gaul, and other fine decorated beakers from production centres in the Lower Rhine, particularly around Cologne. It seems that these and similar imported products were more common in London than the imports of the earlier period. Like samian, and perhaps for the same reasons, the black beakers seem to have been made in standard sizes unlike those from the Highgate kilns.

The same quay groups from the St Magnus House site also contain mortaria and other coarse wares from the Eifel region of Germany, and coarse wares from Northern France, perhaps from the region around Amiens. The mortaria, particularly those stamped by the potter Verecundus, are rather larger and denser than most mortaria of British origin, and may have had a specific culinary function. There are no reliable figures for mortarium usage in London during this period, but it may be that Rhineland imports held a significant part of the market, the remainder coming from a variety of British sources.

LATE ROMAN PERIOD

Pottery assemblages of the third and fourth centuries AD are much rarer than those of the early Roman period, those of the third century particularly so, and it is rather difficult to compare the patterns of pottery usage in the two periods. Samian imports effectively ceased towards the middle of the third century, earlier in most parts of the province, and this signalled the end of large-scale pottery imports. The demand for red-slipped table wares continued and was met by regional pottery producers such as those based in the Oxfordshire region. These continued to produce forms loosely based on samian prototypes until the end of the fourth century and can almost be considered as 'British samian'. Although small by the standards of the early samian factories these potteries operated on a larger scale than had been hitherto seen in Britain. Their repertoire included the complete range of fine and coarse wares, including mortaria, and they comprise almost the entire pottery assemblage found on some sites in the immediate hinterland of the kilns.

The pattern of the first and second centuries in the London area was that various sources supplied the different parts of the pottery repertoire. However, the aim of the large regional producers of the late Roman period seems to have been to market as broad a range of wares over as wide a geographical area as possible, with the fine wares and mortaria having the widest distribution. Alongside these larger all-purpose producers, the smaller domestic grey-ware industries still flourished, and the kilns in the Alice Holt-Farnham area were one of these. They supplied a substantial proportion of all the coarse wares in use in London during the later third and fourth centuries, while mortaria and fine wares came from Oxfordshire and other sites such as those in the Nene Valley. Evidence of fine-ware imports is virtually confined to a few sherds of marbled ware from the Rhineland and south-west France and rare red-slipped wares from North Africa. There is no longer evidence of an extensive, large-scale systematic trade in ceramics, such as that indicated by the groups from the St Magnus House site. Most of London's late Roman imported ceramics probably arrived as by-products of traffic in other commodities.

The native pottery industry was therefore considerably influenced by the overseas producers, but the two sources never seem to have been in direct competition. Indeed, the repertoires of each kiln complemented each other, the native kilns concentrating initially on coarse wares and only expanding into fine-ware production in a major way when the supply of imported products was interrupted, for example. This pattern will now be compared and contrasted with that of other manufacturing industries.

Textiles

Written sources, particularly the Edict of Diocletian, imply that capes and rugs were among Britain's leading exports in the Roman period far outweighing the importance of ceramic wares to the economy, but of this trade there is, regrettably, little direct archaeological evidence. Imported luxury items – silk damask and fine linen – are known from upper-class inhumations within lead or stone coffins (Wild 1970, 96; 101) but in London the recovery of textile remains has been confined to more humble deposits, chiefly pits, which generally yield cloth of a lesser quality if any at all. Fragments of only 19 textiles have been excavated from Roman London but this compares with approximately 12 from York and 10 from Colchester. Yet, despite this small number, both native and foreign products can be recognised from all three towns, providing evidence of the expansion in textile trade for which the Romans were responsible.

The size of the Roman empire with its enormous consumer potential and the heavy demands of the army greatly stimulated the output of good-quality

native textile commodities (Fig. 67; Wild 1979, 128). Patterned cloth woven into finished garments and made according to traditional methods was especially favoured abroad, as well as at home. A characteristic example with a herringbone pattern was found in a second-century pit beside the Walbrook in London (Wild 1975, 139). An unusual feature of this piece is the way the cloth was finished, for along its bottom edge is a twisted 'closing cord' rather than a fringe or sewn-in ends. Closing cords were common on garments woven in Mediterranean provinces (Granger-Taylor 1982, 5) but not north of the Alps. Thus it seems that on occasion modifications could be made to accommodate continental taste; but this practice was limited and cloths of customary native design and finish continued to be produced on warp-weighted looms in Britain until the eleventh century.

London's role in the industry seems to have been a minor one and there is evidence only for spinning and tablet-weaving in the town. This was no doubt because weaving remained a predominantly rural craft or was located in long-established centres of population. The importance of London lay in its demand for finished goods. Overseas imports included items woven from wool as well as silk and linen and it is possible tentatively to identify 45 per cent of the textiles excavated from London as being of foreign manufacture. Thus, in a very small way, the London material reflects the increased traffic in textile goods, which was an enduring feature of the Roman world.

Lamps (Pl. 7b)

From at least the seventh century BC onwards in the lands bordering the Mediterranean the principal means of artificial lighting had been small pottery or bronze oil-lamps. Since each lamp gave little more light than a modern candle, a large number would have been required to illuminate an average-sized room; equally, they would have burnt a considerable amount of fuel – generally olive oil, which was easily obtained in Spain, southern Italy,

67 *The Roman army stimulated the demand for British wool products. This cloak, with characteristic lozenge pattern, was woven by Marianne Straub to a design based on late first-century cloth excavated at Vindolanda. Model of Roman Auxiliary soldier in Housesteads Museum, Hadrian's Wall. Reproduced by permission of the Historic Buildings and Monuments Commission.*

Greece and the eastern Mediterranean, but which elsewhere had to be imported.

Lamps were never common in Roman Britain, but London has probably yielded more than any other town, except, perhaps, Colchester. As both places were ports, olive oil – which is too bulky for long-distance carriage overland – would have been more readily available than elsewhere. In the first century BC and the early first century AD the pottery lamp industry of the western Mediterranean seems to have centred in Italy, where it was in the hands of large-scale manufacturers. Mass-production and mass export is shown, for example, by the finding at Porta Crista, off the east coast of Spain, of a wreck whose recognisable cargo consisted almost entirely of lamps stamped C. CLODIVS. By AD 43, however, lamp-manufacture in this region seems to have become a by-product of the major pottery industries, and lamps may have been imported and marketed with cups, beakers, bowls and other fine vessels. Analysis of the clays and comparison with pottery from known sources has shown that nearly all the mid-first-century lamps found in London were made in Gaul: the largest group is from central/southern Gaul, around Lyon, but others were made in the Allier valley to the west and possibly at Montans in the south-west near Toulouse. Lamps of this period were generally coloured with a buff, brown or orange slip, were decorated with a volute around the nozzle, and had an elaborate design on the upper surface often showing a scene from mythology or daily life.

The 50s and 60s saw the introduction of two new types of lamp. One was a plain-nozzled version of the earlier 'volute' form, but it is rarely found in Britain and its circulation seems to have been restricted mainly to Italy and neighbouring provinces. The other was a completely new type, which in the second century was to become by far the most common lamp in Britain and the north-west of the Empire. It was plain and functional, and is generally thought to have developed in Italy, the source of the earliest lamps of this type which have been found in London. Many were marked on the base with the name of the maker or 'factory'. This may have been intended to prevent unauthorised copying, but lamps with the names of north Italian makers were soon being made in Gaul and Germany, and the progressive deterioration in the clarity of the lettering suggests that this was done by illicit casting from originals, rather than in regularly organised branch-workshops (Fig. 68).

68 *Original 'factory' lamps were copied extensively by other manufacturers (see Pl. 7b), but these drawings of stamps on the base of such vessels show casting deteriorated progressively. The FORTIS factory was in north Italy, but fabric analysis shows that only the one on the left is genuine (c50mm diameter). The one in the middle is from France, the other from Germany.*

In fact, as in the first century, there is little doubt that most of the second-century lamps from London were made in the main pottery production-centres, no longer in southern Gaul and Lyon but principally at Lezoux and in the Rhineland around Trier.

Lamps of the traditional type were never made in large numbers in Britain. A factory seems to have operated in Colchester in the middle of the first century but only a very small part of its output reached London. More significant is a group of second-century 'factory lamps' coated with mica so as to give a sparkling finish; some were made in Hertfordshire, others, possibly, in London itself.

There is a further class of lamps rarely found in the Mediterranean but common in Britain, Gaul and Germany, which in London is almost as common as the enclosed type. These are open, figure-of-eight-shaped trays, often with a simple loop-handle, and are usually interpreted as drip-trays. Pottery lamps are messy, since the oil tends to seep out of the nozzle faster than it burns, but although this may have been their original function, in some cases severe sooting suggests that they were themselves used as lamps. Some were imported from the Rhineland, but most of those found in London are poorly made from local clays,

and production-sites are now known around Verulamium, and in the City itself not far from the present St Paul's Cathedral.

Pottery lamps do not seem to have been used in London much later than AD 170–200. Lamp production continued in Italy to the end of the Roman period, but in north-west Europe it finished with the collapse of the Gaulish potteries in the middle of the third century; neither lamps of the traditional enclosed form nor of the open figure-of-eight became part of the repertoire of the late Romano–British industries. This was a direct result, not of technological inadequacy but of the disruption in the supply of fuel oil, which, as shown above, ceased to be imported in the late Roman period. The decline in the production and popularity of lamps which used imported oil is therefore seen as a reflection of changes in the province's overseas contacts brought about by the changing political and military situation in the late Roman period.

Glassware (Pl. 6b)

By contrast, it was technological factors which were principally responsible for changes in the production and distribution of glassware. In the first century AD the glass industry underwent a complete transformation. The discovery that glass could be blown meant that it could be truly mass-produced for the first time, and ensured that it would join pottery, metalware and woodwork as a 'consumer durable' for everyday use. Hitherto most glass had been cast, which was laborious and expensive: enclosed forms had to be built up from coils, open forms required careful grinding and polishing, and because glassmakers liked to use patterns and bright opaque colours to conceal the heaviness of the vessels, the raw metal had to be carefully prepared, often as 'millefiori' rods. The main centres of production seem to have been in Syria and Alexandria, and the repertoire included phials and flasks – which no doubt often contained the perfumes exported from the same region – and small dishes or plates. Vessels of this type are occasionally found in London, but although production probably continued at least as late as AD 50, they may have arrived with their owners as 'antiques', rather than for sale.

Glass-blowing was invented no later than 25–20 BC (Grose 1977, 29), but it was probably not before AD 40–45, when the technique had spread across Italy to Gaul and the Rhineland, that bulk export to the markets of the north-west provinces became possible. In Colchester glass became relatively common as early as the 50s (Harden 1947, 289–90), but in London there is little evidence for it until at least a decade later. For example, on the excavations at 5–12 Fenchurch Street, in the heart of the early city, less than 100gm (0.08 Estimated Vessel Equivalents) was associated with the buildings destroyed in the Boudican revolt and at the GPO Newgate Street site, an area which may have been outside the city boundary for much of the first century, none at all.

On most late first- and second-century sites the traditional 'luxury' vessels, drinking cups and tableware are far outnumbered by a new range of storage forms. Chief among these are circular, square or many-sided bottles, which had capacities ranging from 50cc to over 1250cc (Charlesworth 1966, 40), and globular jars, which were provided with a string rim to hold a loose cover. Almost invariably they were made in a thick, unrefined glass which was naturally coloured bluish-green by iron impurities. There appeared at the same time a range of cheap tablewares – flagons and flasks, in particular – which were made in much the same manner as the storage vessels; but the finest glass of the late first century still adhered to many of the old traditions: 'pillar-moulded' bowls were cast and polished, some vessels were brightly coloured in amber, blue, red or green, and drinking vessels – skyphoi, for example, or the mould-blown beakers which copy repoussé work – were often made in imitation of metalwares. In contrast, during the second and third centuries there came to be much more emphasis on delicate, blown forms, on colourless 'crystal' – particularly for dishes and cups – and on cutting, engraving and surface-decoration with applied trails.

Unfortunately it is rarely possible to identify the exact production-centres. Compositional analyses are less easy to interpret than those of pottery because glass-blowers use large quantities of remelted glass (cullet) rather than raw materials. Distributional analyses, however, suggest that most of the globular or pear-shaped flagons and jars with pushed-in bases were made in Gaul and in the Rhineland, principally, perhaps, at Cologne. The same is true of mould-blown beakers – particularly those decorated with circus scenes, which are rarely found south of the Alps (Price 1978) – and moulds for some of the most common storage bottles have actually been found at Amiens and elsewhere in Gaul. On the other hand, some of the late first-century bowls, jars and bottles in a fine clear blue glass may have been made further afield, in southern Gaul or northern Italy (J. Shepherd, pers. comm.), and an Italian or even, perhaps, an Alexandrian origin is likely for the millefiori dishes.

Late in the second or early in the third century the industry underwent a second major transformation as trading in utilitarian storage vessels virtually came to an end. Third-century glass importers seem to have catered mainly for the 'upper end of the market': cups, flasks, jugs, phials and unguent jars are the most common finds on London sites of this period. At the same time, however, there was a significant increase in the use of window-glass, much of which must have been manufactured locally. This pattern continued until the end of the Roman period, although there was a steady decline in quality. Associated with the late Roman occupation of Building 6 on the Pudding Lane site were several vessels in a poor, bubbly, greenish-clear glass: a flask, a bowl and several beakers or lamps in the conical form which marks the transition to the glass of the Saxon kingdoms.

Ceramic figurines (Fig. 69)

During the second century in particular London imported large numbers of small pottery figurines. The reasons for the expansion of this trade are not yet fully understood but, since aesthetics and religious practice were also involved, they may have been quite different from those ruling the progress of other manufacturing industries.

Terracottas had been especially popular in Greece and Asia Minor in Classical and Hellenistic times (fifth to first centuries BC), generally as children's toys or cheap but often beautifully-produced ornaments or votive offerings for those

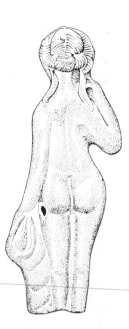

69 *Many white clay figurines were imported into London from Central Gaul during the second century. Of the various gods and mythological figures represented, Venus was by far the most popular; this example, from St Magnus House, was drawn by J. Pearson. The lion and the beautifully-modelled female head (a mother goddess or portrait bust) are much rarer finds, and came from the Pudding Lane sites. Drawn by A. Sutton.*

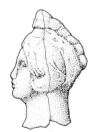

who could not afford stone and bronze (Higgins 1967, xlix). By contrast in the Roman Empire production seems to have been less widespread, particularly in the Mediterranean basin – perhaps because bronze had become very much cheaper (Bailey 1983, 198–9). The industry which developed first in the Allier valley of Central Gaul and probably a little later in the Rhineland was thus remarkable for the scale of its output and the distances travelled by its products. Two factors may have contributed to this: the opportunity for marketing figurines alongside pottery from the same area and the fact that the local white clay produced a much more pleasing, marble-like appearance than the normal buff or red clays.

The figurines are first found on the London waterfront on sites of early second-century date and include a wide range of subjects: birds, a lion, a horse, a bust of a comic boy ('Risus') and a finely-modelled 'portrait' bust. However, the two most common types are the goddess Venus disrobing for her bath (over 50 examples from London) and a Mother Goddess, usually sitting in a basket chair (over 12 examples; Jenkins 1978). The popularity of the Venus figurine was apparently not restricted to London, for over 40 examples were found in an unpacked transit case at Gauting in Germany (M. Rhodes, pers. comm.), but hardly a single example has been found outside Britain, France or Germany (Jenkins 1958). This is surprising, since unlike the cult of the Mother Goddesses, worship of Venus was not restricted to north-west Europe and as the goddess of love and the family she would have been particularly honoured in household shrines. The type itself is based on a well-known Greek statue of the fourth century BC and is a further indication of the appetite of Roman art-collectors. Just as today shops in Rome sell replicas of Michelangelo's sculptures in any size and to suit any pocket, so in ancient times manufacturers produced copies of famous Greek work in stone, bronze or terracotta (Richter 1955, 34–5). To judge by the finds from London, the Gaulish figurine industry did not survive beyond the early third century. This may have been because it was closely associated with the nearby pottery industries, but also, perhaps, because with the growing acceptance of Christianity there was less demand for the traditional mythological subjects. This hypothesis is supported by the fact that the terracotta industry of the eastern provinces died out simultaneously (Higgins 1967).

The changing pattern of traffic in Roman London

This survey has summarised the range of imports known to have reached Roman London, the changing sources from which they came, and something of the inter-relationship between locally available and imported products. Perhaps what is most remarkable is the *quantity* of imports: not merely the odd 'exotic' item – an ivory bracelet, rare glass bowl or marble slab – but commodities such as wine or olive oil which appear to have been imported in bulk so that a 'Roman' way of life could be maintained. Numerous pottery vessels and other manufactured goods partly complemented local products, generally by feeding the 'upper end of the market', and partly replaced them, as when in the second century the supply of Central Gaulish and Rhineland beakers seems to have succeeded those from small north London kilns. Occasionally – most often in the first century – immigrant craftsmen settled in southern Britain to produce Continental-type goods, but except in mortarium-making these enterprises were generally short-lived, so that many manufactured products continued to be transported long distances.

Although a proportion of these imported items, particularly those found near the waterfront, were presumably intended for redistribution within the Province, the majority were probably imported for use in London itself. For example, on some first-century domestic sites near the Forum, imported samian accounts for over one in four of all the pottery vessels found, and on a site at the extreme western edge of the city, as many as one in ten (information P. Tyers). In London households, therefore, samian was commonplace. So were lamps, several of which have been found on nearly every site that has been excavated. No doubt these items were cheaper than elsewhere in Britain because high overland transport costs did not have to be added to the basic price.

The long-distance movement of foodstuffs and manufactured goods was in fact a tradition of the ancient Mediterranean world, and in this respect the Roman Empire was heir to an existing system. The sheer scale of imperial needs – in marble building materials or grain for the City of Rome, for example – led to increasing imperial monopoly of some supply-networks and, in a very few cases, to direct control of them. However, there is little evidence to suggest that the *negotiatores* who arranged transportation and handled most of the business were anything other than private individuals (d'Arms 1981; Hopkins 1980).

Two major factors, one geographical and the other political, combined to promote long-distance traffic. The geographical factor was that almost without exception the cities of Greece, Asia Minor, North Africa and southern Italy lay on the coast and large quantities of material could therefore be moved easily between them by ship. Inland sites were comparatively isolated because overland transport costs were high. However, use of the English Channel and the rivers of north-west Europe meant that at least for a time a fundamentally Mediterranean system could be extended to include most of Gaul and the Rhineland, London and other sites in south-east Britain. It is remarkable that in the first and second centuries London was almost exclusively supplied with quern- and millstones from Gaul or Germany; native British quernstones – Millstone Grit, for example – seem hardly to have been used at all before the third and fourth centuries.

The political factor was that from the eighth century BC onwards it became normal for cities to send out colonies to all parts of the known world. The initial reason may have been land-hunger, but increasingly it became a device for securing newly conquered terrain. Citizen colonies of discharged legionaries were still being founded in the first century AD, but by this time the chief instrument of government had become the army and an organised 'civil service' assigned tours of duty abroad. Nevertheless, the effect was the same: the 'colonists' created a demand for goods to be transported long distances from their home towns so that they could continue to live in the manner to which they were accustomed.

This factor may have been especially relevant in the case of Roman London, for as the seat of the governor and procurator, the city was arguably the most cosmopolitan town in Britain, the most 'Roman' and the most filled with wealthy individuals. This can be appreciated by study of the surviving epigraphy, which from north of the Thames alone provides the names of over 70 persons. Significantly, not one is a proven merchant or trader, but they do include a provincial governor, an imperial procurator, five imperial freedmen ('senior civil servants') and nine soldiers, one of whom was a centurion and the others legionaries. All were wealthy enough to erect, or be commemorated by, major stone monuments, and

70 *The cosmopolitan population of London. A. Alfidus Olussa was one of several Greeks known to have lived in London. He was born in Athens and died aged 70. This tombstone was set up near Tower Hill by his heir. Photo: copyright British Museum.*

York
Chester
BRITANNIA
London
Zwammerdam
Domburg
Pommeroeul
Cologne
Amiens
pottery
Eifel
quernstones
Trier
LUGDUNENSIS
BELGICA
Mosel
Rhine
Loire
Saône
pottery
Allier
wine
Lezoux
Lyon
Rhône
Toulouse
GALLIA NARBONENSIS
Clunia
marble
Narbonne
Arles
Marseilles
GALLIA CISALPINA
marble
Carrara
PANNONIA
River Danube
TARRACONENSIS
fish sauce
Tiber
Rome
CAMPANIA
wine
fish sauce
BAETICA
wine
olive oil
fish sauce
wine
fish sauce
Constantinople
Thasos
marble
Skyros
Euboea
PHRYGIA
Athens
Rhodes
SYRIA
olive oil
Leptis Magna
Alexandria
Nile
0
700km

71 *Roman provinces and towns mentioned in the text, with main sources of some of the products imported to Roman London indicated.*

there are, in addition, a further eight 'civilians' – both men and women – whose nomenclature shows them to have been full Roman citizens, and several others who may have been.

The *Romanitas* of this class is emphasised by the fact that probably only two truly Celtic (and perhaps British) names are known. One of them, Dagobitus, significantly gave his daughter the Roman name of Grata. Others, including the procurator Classicianus and, probably, the third-century governor M. Martiannius Pulcher (Birley 1979, 124), may have been Celtic in origin, but were Roman citizens of long standing. It is a pity that the actual home towns are recorded of only two individuals: A. Alfidius Olussa, born at Athens (Fig. 70), and Ulpius Silvanus, a soldier enlisted (if not born) at Orange in Gallia Narbonensis. But to judge by her name Aurelia Eucarpia was also born in Greece or Asia Minor, and several graffiti – one of which ('orator'), perhaps itself a personal name, was scratched on wall plaster from the warehouses at Pudding Lane and another ('Hector') was inscribed on a child's shoe (*Britannia* vi (1975), 287) – show that Greek was spoken and written in London. The birthplaces of the other recorded persons are unfortunately impossible to establish from their nomenclature.

The Mediterranean exchange system in foodstuffs and manufactured goods, which had developed for these reasons and into which, by extension, London was integrated at the time of its foundation, seems at that time to have embraced mainly Gaul, Spain and north/central Italy. The nodal point was probably Narbonne, for this city could manage the coastal trade in foodstuffs from Spain and wine and manufactured goods from Italy, could combine these with the products of the rapidly-developing wine and manufacturing industries of Narbonensis itself, and could funnel them northwards along the Rhone to the Rhine or to Bordeaux and the Garonne. This system had probably begun to grow in the second and early first centuries BC, when Spain and Gallia Cisalpina became Roman provinces, but it had reached maturity in the time of Augustus (31 BC–AD 14), when all Gaul had been settled. The prosperity of Narbonensis from Augustan times onwards can still be seen in monuments such as the temples, theatres and amphitheatres of Arles, Nîmes or Orange.

By the early second century, however, the pattern seems to have changed slightly as London became ever more closely linked with the three Gauls and Germany. At the same time contact with Cornwall and Dorset may have increased; stone, tin and shale had been brought from here in the first century, but the extensive use of Black-Burnished pottery dates from after c130. Spain and Narbonensis probably remained the principal exporters of wine, olive oil and their associated commodities, but increased contact with central Gaul and the Rhineland is shown by the preponderance of pottery, lamps and glassware from that region. One of the most important elements in the system was perhaps the city of Lyon, which has yielded many inscriptions of *nautae*, 'sailors' (*CIL* xiii, index xii), and which commands the route to the Mediterranean via the Rhône, the route to Germany via the Saône and the route to north-western Gaul via the Allier and Loire.

The decline of north/central Italy as a source of London's manufactured goods can be traced back long into the first century, for it was never a major exporter of pottery, only of glass and, for a short period between c75 and 100, of lamps. In fact, during the second century it seems that Italy was becoming part of a second, more southerly regional trade-network in commodities and manufactured goods that embraced Spain and north Africa. At the same time, a long-distance supply of marble was established with the Aegean and Asia Minor, largely supplanting the use of Italian Carrara for the most fashionable work. London's peripheral contact with these systems during the second century is represented by the occurrence of Greek Island and Asiatic marble, and by the occasional finding of African olive oil amphoras.

Another major change seems to have occurred by the middle of the third century. In spite of the relatively rare survival of late Roman deposits on archaeological sites in the City, it now seems clear that the population density was much lower than in the first and second centuries. Indeed, the sites of many buildings seem to have been covered by a cultivated 'garden' soil, although continued activity in the town and the surrounding area is attested by evidence from the harbourside settlement and the extramural cemeteries (Bentley and Pritchard 1983).

There is also considerably less archaeological evidence of imported goods in the late Roman period. Although this must obviously be related to the dearth of well-preserved archaeological deposits of this date, it seems nevertheless that the decline in the number of imports is not directly proportional to the decline in the number of inhabitants, but rather that the range of imports was considerably curtailed. Pottery lamps are never found, glass bottles and common glass storage vessels seldom. Imported pottery is rare and the bulk of London's vessels, both kitchen- and tablewares, came from large, newly developed industries in Britain. Two lines of communication became increasingly important: the Thames westwards, bringing pottery from Oxfordshire and Surrey, and the east coast to the Thames estuary, bringing millstones and jet ornaments from Yorkshire, pottery from the Nene Valley. Coins from mints such as Thessalonica in northern Greece occasionally reveal far-flung contacts and amphoras continued to bring olive oil and perhaps dates and 'exotic' foodstuffs, mainly from the eastern Mediterranean (though in comparison with earlier times they are uncommon and may have reached a much smaller section of the population).

If true, this decrease in imported material would at first sight seem surprising, because at the same time Britain became increasingly linked with the administration of northern Europe. The reforms of Diocletian created a system of regional provincial government, and in the fourth century Britain was

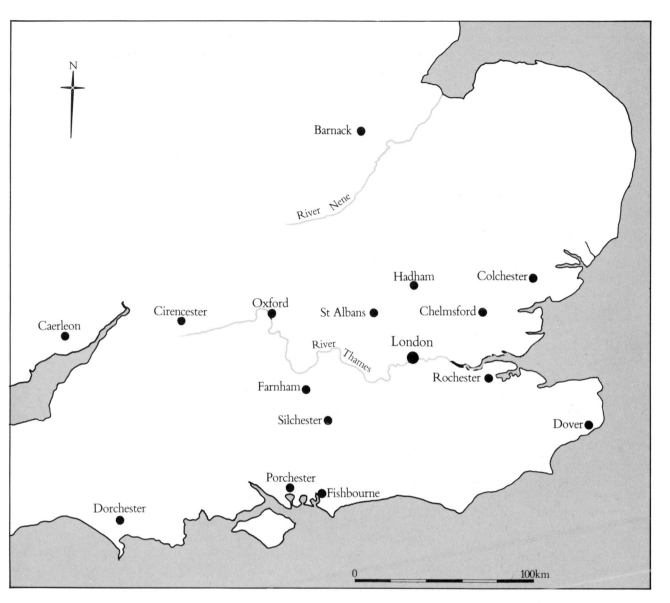

72 *Part of the Roman province of Britannia, showing location of places mentioned in the text.*

integrated into a large 'diocese' controlled by the Praetorian Prefect of the Gauls. Similarly, the establishment of field armies facilitated the movement of soldiers between provinces and for a period at the end of the third century a frontier commander was apparently responsible for both sides of the English Channel.

But in reality these arrangements created a geographical and political unit quite different from that which had fostered the long-distance traffic of the ancient Mediterranean world in the centuries before Christ. There was no continuous waterway to connect the main centres of population, and goods continually had to be unloaded and transferred to seagoing ship, river barge, cart or pack-animal. As a result the centres producing manufactured goods became smaller and increasingly confined their distribution to local markets. At the same time, as a large portion of the army became permanently established on the perimeter of the Empire, the systems supplying it were slowly but drastically changed. The *Notitia Dignitatum* records that weapons and specialised equipment were produced in a small number of factories distributed throughout the Empire and administered by the Praetorian Prefects, but many of the staple foodstuffs seem to have been provided overwhelmingly by farms in the vicinity of the forts and fortresses (Manning 1975a).

By 369 this could be laid down as 'policy' by the emperors Valentinian and Valens (*Codex Theodosianus* vii.4.15) and it had two important consequences. The first was that in frontier provinces resources and manpower were gradually diverted to the countryside near the frontiers themselves, where – in Britain from the late second century onwards – a local infrastructure of trackways, farm-buildings and villages slowly sprang up; moreover, as local recruitment became normal, demand would have slackened for the olive-oil, wine and amphora-borne commodities typical of Mediterranean living. The second consequence was an increasing tendency for the imperial administration to arrange for goods to be transported directly from the supplier to the consumer (Whittaker 1983) obviating the need for *negotiatores* and other 'middlemen'. In view of the size of the army in Britain, the overall effect may have been a decline in the importation of foodstuffs, a growing separation of the south-east from the north and west, and a reduction in the function of large urban centres as the collecting and redistribution points of large consignments of goods.

Political developments were probably even more influential in the long run. In the first and second centuries the Roman administration had actively fostered a system of local government based on Mediterranean-style towns. Magistrates and members of the *ordo* (tribal council) were legally required to live in the town and the attractiveness of a town seems to have been judged by its adherence to Classical precepts. In the third and especially in the fourth centuries, however, there was a vast development of the imperial civil service, so that tribal self-government was largely replaced by direct administration. This would have left the local magnates free to concentrate on their rural estates – as, indeed, is suggested by the steady growth of country houses, not only in west and north Britain, but in other outlying provinces such as Pannonia (Thomas 1964, 389–90) – and would have removed the compulsion to maintain a way of life which was based on the Classical model and was dependent on Mediterranean imports. Indeed, by this time the imperial bureaucrats who managed the north-western provinces were themselves nearly all native to the area (Matthews 1975, 41–9); Rome and the ancient cities of the Mediterranean seaboard became increasingly introverted and, after the accession of Constantine, the centre of power began to shift eastwards, ultimately to reside in Byzantium.

The political geography of the late Roman empire was thus quite different from that of the early empire. In the west the change from the old to the new probably came quite suddenly in the middle of the third century. Overrunning of whole provinces by barbarians, marauding by pirates and many rounds of debilitating civil war brought an end to established but now frail systems of communication. In London, perhaps one of the more important ports in the early province, analysis of the imported material suggests that the effects were particularly severe; but, to judge from the evidence of contraction of settlement within the city, they were the culmination of a process which had begun nearly a century earlier.

BUILDING ON THE WATERFRONT

The study of buildings is obviously a central part of urban archaeology. For example, an assessment of the form, structure and architectural pretensions of buildings can say much about function and ownership. Taking a wider perspective, the relationship between buildings and the layout and development of the *insulae* themselves (square or rectangular plots bounded by streets) will reflect the degree to which an area was or was not affected by centrally controlled town planning. If all these strands are tied together, it is sometimes possible for the archaeologist to draw the broad outline of urban life, noting the changing pattern of prosperity, and assessing the often contrasting roles of property owners and occupiers.

Obviously, the strength of any conclusions suggested by such a study will be tempered by the quality of the evidence, or, more specifically, the quality of the record of that raw data. As already discussed in Chapter 1, the main elements of London's Roman waterfront have been investigated by many people using different methods over many years, and so the field observations are of varying reliability. Nevertheless, as with much archaeological work, the bringing together of such disparate information often produces a pattern not discernible in the individual elements: the whole is greater than the sum of the parts. It is suggested that there is now sufficient evidence to make a valid assessment of life on the waterfront of Roman London.

In Chapter 2, the broad outline of waterfront development was summarised and its ambitious scale demonstrated. In this chapter it is argued that the project integrated the construction of massive timber quays with the establishment of a series of artificial terraces, the provision of a regular system of roads and drains, and the erection of buildings within this well-defined framework (Fig. 74). First, consideration will be given to major topographical elements which can be shown to reflect a carefully conceived plan for the area as a whole. It is then suggested that the waterfront was subjected to unified 'town-planning' measures which clearly raises the question of ownership. Next, the development of two specific building complexes within this scheme are analysed, to focus attention on two other important questions, the responsibilities of the occupants of waterfront buildings, and the persistence of activity in the harbour area.

Terracing the hillside

Before any major first-century building was erected in the waterfront area under consideration, the Romans converted the sloping terrain into a series of level terraces rising up the hillside parallel to the river (Fig. 74b). The lowest of the terraces, which were built out over the foreshore, were revetted with massive baulks of timber, while the higher terraces were faced with masonry walls along their southern edges. Depending on position, the terraces were either negative, ie cut into the hillside, or positive, ie the ground was artificially raised with dumps of earth and refuse. Both types seem to have incorporated a lattice of timber beams laid onto the ground to improve the stability. Evidence was found for several terraces of different widths at differing levels, but both the widths and levels change considerably during the three centuries or so of Roman occupation on the waterfront. To the east of the bridge the lower two terraces were c12m wide north-south, at $c+2$m OD and $c+2.5$m OD respectively when originally laid out, with evidence for a third at $c+3.5$m OD to the north. By the end of the Roman period the level of the lower terrace had been raised by over 1m, and its width increased to c50m north-south by building out into the river. In the west of the study area the pattern is less clear, but the lowest terrace, occupied by Buildings B, C, and D, may have been at $+3.5$ to $+4$m OD and up to 24m wide initially.

That the formation of these terraces, the construction of the associated buildings and the provision of services were all part of the same integrated development plan is clear. For example, to the east of the bridge at the end of the first-century

Buildings 1 and 2 lay parallel to the waterfront on the lowest of the terraces, but their massive northern walls formed the revetment for the second terrace. The foundations of the buildings had obviously been designed to utilise the remains of the partially dismantled landing-stage which a timber quay directly replaced in cAD 90 (Chapter 5) and to accommodate the main drainage channel which passed between them. Moreover, the aperture for the same drain in the south face of the quay was designed as an integral part of that structure, and where the drain passed through the revetment for the second terrace it was spanned by a masonry arch which was structurally integrated with the northern walls of both Buildings 1 and 2 (Pl. 5a). These observations demonstrate that the construction and function of all these elements were integrated.

Drainage

Several drains were laid at right angles across the lines of the terraces, and therefore formed important topographical sub-divisions. Although the body of the main drain on the Pudding Lane site was replaced at least twice, its line was respected by a succession of buildings on all the lower terraces, and it remained in use for over 300 years. When the drain was deliberately backfilled in the late fourth century, water-laid silts started to accumulate to the north of the terrace wall, the rear wall of Buildings 1 and 2. This suggests that the drain served a dual role, not only removing waste from neighbouring structures but also canalising the flow of ground water which collected on the terraces or rose on the spring line.

Near the south-west corner of Building 1 was another timber-lined drain. It ran at an angle across the metalled area in front of the horrea, possibly to avoid the bridge pier which lay to the south, but it must have extended northwards between the bridge approach road and Building 1.

Between Buildings 2 and 7 two separate sequences of east-west aligned timber-lined drains

were recorded, one immediately south of Building 7, the other immediately north of Building 2. It is known that the latter must have drained eastwards, but that the former did not extend across the external metalled area to the north of Building 8. Because no continuation of the southern external wall of Building 7 was recorded in the trench immediately to the east it is argued that the eastern wall of the building must have been situated between the two trenches, possibly on a very similar alignment to the eastern external wall of Building 2 (Fig. 17a). It therefore seems likely that the two sequences of east-west drains disgorged into a south-flowing drain immediately to the east of both buildings, but beyond the limit of controlled excavations.

A substantial timber-lined drain was recorded on the Miles Lane site separating Building B which was constructed on the lower terrace, from Building A, which extended northwards up the hillside across the line of the terrace divisions (Fig. 75). Like those to the east, this drain remained in use for a very long time, and it is quite likely that it also served a dual function, canalising natural spring water and serving as a drain for waste and effluent.

Among the varied types of drain construction found on the sites, channels incorporating planked walls (Fig. 75) and sections of dug-out timbers (Fig. 59; Pl. 1) are represented, together with masonry channels and one example of an enclosed hollowed-out tree-trunk drain. This diversity probably reflects the different dates at which the drains were rebuilt and the contemporary availability of resources, and does not invalidate the conclusion that the drainage system was initially conceived as part of an integrated plan.

Buildings and streets

Many of the buildings which initially occupied the terraces were clearly an integral part of the same waterfront development plan since their massive northern walls often formed the retaining revetment for the adjacent higher terrace. However, this pattern of buildings laid out parallel to the river was broken by the presence of building ranges stepped down across the line of the terrace walls. One such complex, Building A, was recorded in detail on the Miles Lane site (Fig. 12). Its southern room was probably open fronted and led out onto the quayside. The other rooms were laid out at different levels, and since there was no evidence for communicating doorways, access would have been

73 *Part of a substantial masonry and brick building built on the waterfront in the second century. The culverted drains shown here with a 2 × 100mm scale carried water from a bath block into the main drain which disgorged directly into the Thames.*

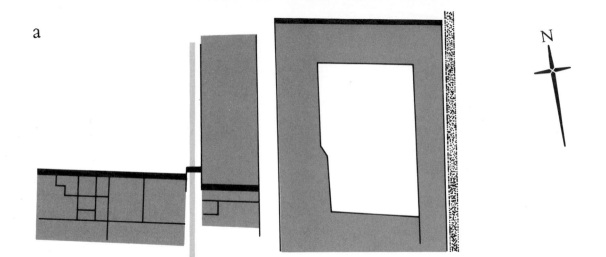

a

N

74 *The plan for the London waterfront from* **a** *the Cannon Street Station area in west to* **b** *the Miles Lane and Pudding Lane excavations in the east. The steeply sloping hillside incorporated terraces, defined by the masonry walls shown here in thick black lines, roads, drains, and buildings aligned alternately north-south and east-west.*

gained not from the west (where the main drain lay), but from a street or yard to the east. Unfortunately, that area lay beyond the limit of controlled excavation beneath the approach to modern London Bridge.

Another possible building positioned at right angles to the waterfront and running north across the main terraces may be represented by a substantial length of north-south masonry wall observed in the 1920s during the construction of Regis House (Waddington 1931, 5 and Marsh 1981). Gravel metalling seen against its eastern face may have been part of the main north-south road leading to the Roman bridge. Evidence for a similar range, Building 8, was recorded some 80m further east. Only the north-east corner was found, but its alignment (which differed from that of the first-century horrea Buildings 1 and 2 to the west), was similar to that of the new horrea constructed to the south soon after the second-century fire (see Chapter 2, Fig. 17a). At least one of the internal walls was decorated with painted wall-plaster, perhaps suggesting that Building 8 may have had a domestic rather than a commercial function. The building cannot have been more than 7m wide and therefore probably extended southwards over the terrace divisions. The substantial area of metalling recorded against its eastern face could represent a north-south street leading down to the river.

This pattern of 'terrace buildings' laid out parallel to the river alternating with buildings running north-south over one or more of the artificial terraces seems to extend west of the study area to the sites near Bush Lane and Cannon Street Station (Fig. 74a). This is the complex of structures thought to represent part of the provincial Governor's Palace (Marsden 1975). The range of rooms interpreted as the 'south wing' of the palace shared a common rear wall which also served as the revetment for the terrace to the north, the ground level being up to 3m higher to the north than to the south. To the east of this wall two separate north-south aligned ranges were recorded. The one interpreted as the 'east wing' of the palace lay on a terrace c3m higher than the 'south wing' and was not structurally integrated with it. The other lay further to the east forming a separate building. Like Building A to the east but unlike the structures to the west, this Roman building was gradually stepped down the hillside and may have been bounded on its eastern side by a north-south running road (Marsden 1975, 58–60).

A recognisable pattern of buildings, drains and streets was therefore laid out over the waterfront terraces during the late first century, with buildings aligned alternately north-south and east-west. It is just possible that the Cannon Street Station complex interpreted as the southern and eastern ranges of a palace may simply represent a continuation of the pattern recorded in more detail on, for example, the Miles Lane site immediately to the east (Fig. 74).

What is certain is that this major urban development, extending along the waterfront for several hundred metres east-west, integrated major elements such as the laying-out of terraces and the provision of a drainage system. As might be

b

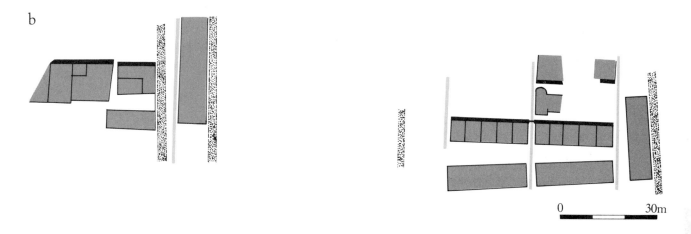

0   30m

75 *This major drain excavated on the Miles Lane*
site was revetted with timber posts and planks.
Looking north-west, 0.5m scale.

expected, there were regular elements in the ensuing pattern. For example, the streets discussed above were laid out *c*80m east and 80m west of the bridge approach road. However, there were considerable variations in the levels and dimensions of the terraces, in the form and function of the buildings, and in the type and spacing of the drains. It would seem that the overall design of the plan was frequently modified to take maximum advantage of local topographical variations. As a result, the terraces were of irregular size to accommodate variations on the slope of the hillside, and although drains were required at frequent intervals, these too did not need to be regular, but made use of existing stream beds wherever possible.

Such a massive undertaking is unlikely to have been a private enterprise, and, although obviously centrally controlled, was not part of a military exercise – in the sense that it served no defensive purpose. It is suggested that the waterfront area in general was developed as part of an official development programme.

However, once laid out, individual buildings and areas seem to have been managed or rented out to various individuals or institutions, and modified accordingly. Thereafter, co-ordinated redevelopment of buildings seems to have occurred only after major fires or waterfront extensions. At such times it could be suggested that responsibility reverted once more to an official body with wide ranging powers. An examination of the subsequent history of specific buildings on the waterfront bears out the conclusion that, for the most part, different agencies used, managed or maintained the buildings.

76 *Section through the remains of a culverted drain beneath Building A, looking south-west, 2 × 100mm scale.*

The development of Building 2: a warehouse transformed

When originally constructed in the late first century, Building 2 seems to have served as a waterfront horrea (Pl. 1; Figs. 77, 78). In Chapter 6 it was shown that its form changed after a mid-second-century fire which made reconstruction necessary. This suggests a corresponding change in the function of the building to that of a shop, with the new structures to the south interpreted as the replacement horrea. Since the general nature of the structural modifications was the same in each bay or room of Building 2 it seems likely that this was a unified and deliberate redevelopment rather than a piecemeal affair (Figs. 77a, 77b, 78a, 78b). However, each bay was now provided with floors of differing materials, perhaps partly the result of the introduction of solid partition walls preventing direct access between rooms (Fig. 77c). This may imply that differing activities were carried on in each room, or that each was managed by, and perhaps rented out to, different people. During the next two centuries, differing rates of redevelopment and differing patterns of use and wear resulted in floors of adjoining rooms being separated by as much as 0.6m in height (Figs. 71c–f; Figs. 78c, 78d; 80). In general, the evidence points to domestic occupation in many of the rooms, though for a brief period there is also tentative evidence for quasi-industrial activity. This remarkable sequence of waterfront activity in which a building was transformed from a horrea into a shop and then into domestic 'apartments', is obviously of considerable significance, and the final stage in the process clearly merits more detailed examination.

BUILDING 2 IN THE THIRD CENTURY

By the early third century the waterfront had been advanced c33m south of the line of the late first-century quay (Fig. 17b). The main north-south drain west of Building 2 was reset 1m higher to take account of the greater distance its contents had to be carried to reach the river. A square collecting tank at the foot of the west wall of Building 2 disgorged into the drain, which passed between two of a series of rectangular arch or column foundations to the south (Fig. 77d). These substantial features represent a major modification to the south wall of Building 2, perhaps suggesting a colonnaded portico in front of the entrances to the individual rooms. There was evidence for a solid wall rather than for a colonnade at the eastern end, where the differently aligned north wall of the new

horrea came to within a few centimetres of the Building 2 frontage. In addition, the internal partition walls were altered at the same time. In the westernmost room of Building 2 (Room 1), the south end of the bay wall was cut back over 1m to a point exactly midway between the original north wall and the newly constructed colonnade of the building. An east-west aligned beam slot at this point separated the brickearth and mortar surfaces in the north from the sand and rubble surfaces to the south, but it is uncertain whether the slot supported a solid partition wall. The partition wall separating Rooms 4 and 5 of the building was completely removed and replaced by a free-standing brick column at the south end. A raised timber floor was laid out over the enlarged floor space to the north of this column, sealing the remains of the levelled wall, while brickearth and mortar surfaces occupied the area to the south of it. It is uncertain how or whether these two areas were divided.

These modifications reflect two very different sets of needs and responsibilities. The construction of the new colonnaded south wall, evidence for which also existed to the south of Building 1, clearly represents large scale redevelopment, probably at the initiative of the *owner* of the property. Significantly, there is both stratigraphic and dating evidence to relate this activity directly to the third-century advance of the waterfront to the south. By contrast, the subsequent alterations to the form of Rooms 1, 4 and 5 seem to reflect the needs of the *occupier* of the individual room rather than another extensive waterfront redevelopment plan.

BUILDING 2 IN THE FOURTH CENTURY

In the later Roman period, each room within the building seems to have developed independently, and the precise interrelationship of the discrete sequences cannot be established. The partition wall separating Rooms 4 and 5 was re-erected and a series of brickearth, mortar and *opus signinum* floors was laid in Room 5 extending westwards and to the south of Room 5. However, these surfaces did not extend into Room 4 itself, in which the contemporary surviving surface was 0.6m lower, although the presence of several post-holes groups may represent a raised timber floor which had subsequently been removed (Fig. 80).

During the mid- to late fourth century the drain which separated Buildings 1 and 2 was deliberately infilled with earth and rubbish and levelled over with ragstones packed in silt. At the same time the

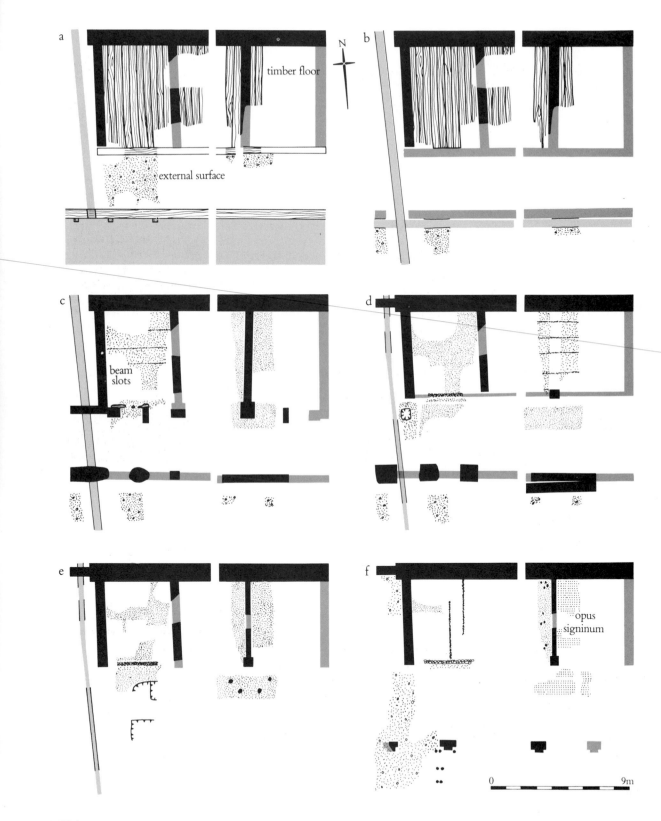

a

timber floor

N

external surface

b

c

beam
slots

d

e

f

opus
signinum

0   9m

134

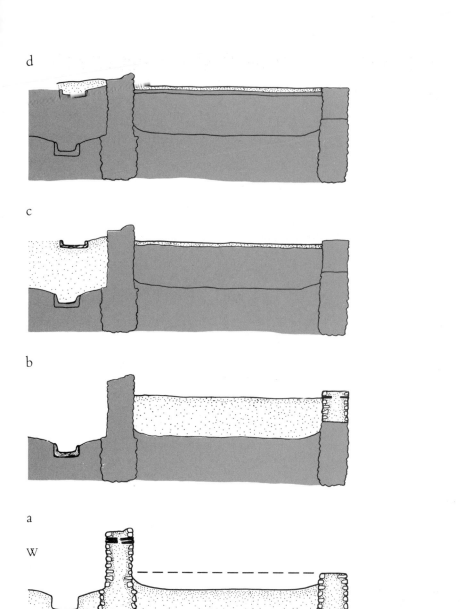
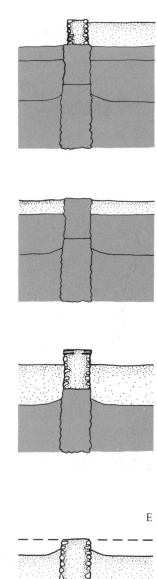

d

c

b

a

W   E

0 ▬▬▬▬▬▬ 3m

77 *A warehouse transformed: composite plan of the development of Building 2, recorded on sites to east and west of Pudding Lane.*
a *and* **b** *Uniform development in first and second century,*
c *to* **f** *increasingly separate development in late second, third, mid- and late fourth century. See Fig. 78.*

78 *Composite section across Building 2 showing accumulation of surfaces:*
a *late first century: dashed lines show suggested height at which timber floor functioned;*
b *mid-second century,*
c *early third century,*
d *late fourth century.*

79 *The division between two identical timber-floored bays of Building 2, looking north, recorded just east of Pudding Lane in 1980. Compare Fig. 80.*

80 *By the late fourth century, these two bays of Building 2 had developed quite differently, with a timber floor represented by slots to west, and an* opus signinum *surface to east.*

superstructure over the rectangular foundations of the south wall was removed and a series of sub-surface features and pits, the function of which is not known, was dug between the robbed south wall and the rooms to the north. Since surfaces were still being laid in these it is argued that, at least at this phase, there must have been a solid partition wall over the beam slot which separated the two areas. Contemporary with the pits and sub-surface features in the southern area were a range of cut features and post-holes at the eastern end of Building 2. Traces of slag and ash, possibly suggesting industrial activity, were recorded on one of the surfaces in Room 5.

In the late fourth century (Fig. 77f), the partition walls were robbed down to the level of the contemporary surfaces leaving the external walls still standing. This probably happened at the same time as the careful levelling of the walls of Building 8 and the deliberate pulling down of the walls of Building 7. A rubble-packed slot probably represents the south wall of the building at this stage, while contemporary with it, in what had been Room 1, were the patchy remains of a sequence up to six more surfaces, the earliest one of which contained a coin of Constantius II (AD 348–51). A joist and plank floor extended east over the levelled remains of the partition wall separating Rooms 1 and 2 but it is not clear whether this floor functioned with the six or so surfaces to its west, or whether it represents a later sub-surface feature truncating the floor sequence. What is certain is that both the timber floor and the surfaces functioned within a building that was by then at least 350 years old. Subsequently, a deposit of dark grey silt over 1m thick sealed the levelled wall, the slots for the floor joists and the slot representing the southern wall, but the main external walls survived even above this deposit.

At the eastern end of the building, development was slightly different. The *opus signinum* floor was worn and decayed, suggesting either considerable use or, more probably, exposure to the elements for a time. Traces of a brazier, erected over this worn floor, were found in the north-west corner of Room 5. This may suggest some temporary squatter occupation on a building that, by then, was at least partly derelict. These traces, the worn floor, and the much lower but contemporary surface in Room 4 were all sealed by a thick deposit of dark grey silt, very similar to that recorded in Rooms 1 and 2. As at the west end of the building however, the main

external wall to the north was left standing above the level of this deposit. It is interesting to note that the external walls must have been still visible in the mid- to late Saxon period since their positions influenced the siting of buildings and pits. The northern wall was retained even after the Great Fire in 1666 and formed the foundations for the southern side of Kings Head Alley until its destruction in 1980.

The development of Building 2 may now be summarised. As the waterfront moved to the south, the function of Buildings 1 and 2 changed from one of mixed storage and marketing to one more specifically of selling goods (Chapter 6). The third- to fifth-century occupation of Building 2 described in this chapter is characterised by increasingly divergent development in all the rooms. This may be associated with the final advance of the Roman waterfront in the early third century (see Chapter 2 and Fig. 17) which left Building 2, originally constructed as quayside horrea, stranded 37m north of the riverfront. The buildings expanded when the early third-century quay was constructed and may still have had a variety of commercial functions, probably based around selling and marketing rather than storage. With the decline in the commercial use of the harbour area, the buildings contracted back to their original size and, now enclosed on all four sides, may have been used for living in or, at one stage, small workshops. Throughout this long development, the major alterations seem to be associated with major changes on the waterfront as a whole, suggesting an 'official' interest. By contrast, the subsequent pattern of minor modifications to the individual rooms of the property may reflect the needs of the occupiers themselves.

Building 6 and the late Roman revival

The development of the complex labelled Building 6 (Fig. 81), which may have begun life as a small inn, adds considerably to the story of mid- to late Roman waterfront activity. The structure was established in the mid-second century, and saw several major alterations, the latest one of which was after cAD 370. As such, it extends the picture of the demise of commercial activity in the area presented by the development of the horrea on the lower terrace, and complements the evidence of late Roman residential occupation provided by the buildings on such sites as the old Coal Exchange (Marsden 1980, 151–5; 180–6) and on the eastern side of the White Tower (Parnell *et al* 1982, 105–13).

It is thought that the terrace to the north of the late first-century quay east of the bridge may once have been occupied by timber horrea (cf Figs. 14, 17a). These had been cleared away after a fire had damaged several structures in the vicinity in the mid-second century. Subsequently, as part of a major new waterfront development, a masonry and tile walled building was established on the site, of which part of the apsidal-ended west wing was exposed in the recent controlled excavation (Figs. 81a, 82; Pl. 5b).

The complex was *c*8m wide north-south, but its east-west length is unknown (Fig. 81a). At the northern end, the wall survived 1m high, the internal face and floor of which were finished principally in plain white tesserae, although a thin band of orange tesserae ran around the foot of the wall above the watertight quarter-round moulding (Pl. 5b). Although this feature bears a superficial resemblance to the *nymphaneum* in the court of the House of Neptune at Pompeii (Feder 1978, 98–9) it is perhaps more likely to represent a plunge bath. Such elaborate baths are relatively rare in Britain, but have been found in Colchester (Hull 1958, 208; Pl. 32) and in the villa at Wingham in Kent (Dowker 1882) for example. The floor of the London bath was sunk only *c*0.15m below the internal surface of the building, and so its southern wall must have been raised above this level, the bath being entered from the south by a short flight of steps. This southern wall had been observed and bodily removed in 1833 when a large square hole

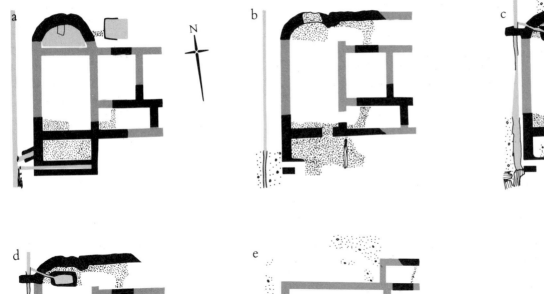
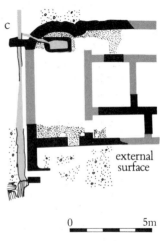
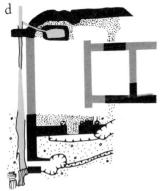
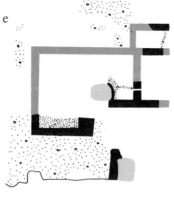

external surface

0   5m

81 *Development of a part of Building 6:*
a *initially built with bath and latrine in mid-second century:*
b *and* **c** *modified in third and early fourth centuries;*
d *partially collapsed in the mid-fourth century;*
e *rebuilt after* cAD 370.

82 *Apsidal-ended plunge bath with 0.5m scale in mid-second-century Building 6 recorded just west of Pudding Lane. See Pl. 5b.*

was dug in the middle of the Roman building to insert a cess-pit (*Gentlemen's Magazine* 1834, 95–6; Merrifield 1965, 285). It was noted that beneath the floor a tiled culvert ran southwards, and presumably connected with a similar feature, found on the controlled excavation, which disgorged into the main timber-lined north-south drain to the west of the building (Fig. 73).

The remains of a second tiled culvert were found in the southern room, running east-west into the same drain (Pl. 8a; Fig. 73). The base was over 1m wide and the channel seems to have been enclosed within a tile 'bench' of which only part of the west end survived. The form of this feature, together with the presence of brown organic staining along the line of the water course itself, suggests that it was a latrine. The type is well known from such sites as Housesteads on Hadrian's Wall. The presence of a prestigious plunge bath and a substantial latrine within the same range suggests that part of a bathblock was represented, the rest of which lay beyond the eastern limit of excavation. Since it is smaller than

the public bath buildings already recorded in London (Marsden 1976; Merrifield 1983, 84–7), but arguably larger than that required for a purely domestic dwelling, it may have been attached to a waterfront inn. A similar interpretation is offered for the third-century building and bath suite excavated on the old Coal Exchange site (Marsden 1980, 155), some 100m east of Building 6. Both these buildings seem to have been sited on the hillside to take advantage of the plentiful water supply found on the spring line.

BUILDING 6 IN THE THIRD AND FOURTH CENTURIES
After the final advance of the Roman waterfront in the early third century, Building 6 was rebuilt in a radically different form (Fig. 81b). The bath and latrine were infilled and the internal floor level of the building was raised to c + 3.8m OD. A corridor was erected in the north, doorways were cut in the northern and southern walls and new floors were laid, including a black-and-white mosaic (Pl. 8b). The southern door from that room led into a small courtyard at a lower level with more rooms leading off it, built against the back wall of Building 2. On the western side, the culverts were blocked and no longer disgorged into the main north-south drain, which was itself enclosed and set at a higher level, taking the form of a hollowed-out tree trunk. The

transformation of the bath block into a suite of rooms and corridors suggests that the building was now a private residence. This major change seems to form part of a wider redevelopment which affected most of the waterfront at this date.

Domestic occupation continued for a substantial period, as the six layers of wall plaster in the southern range of rooms testify. There were some modifications however (Fig. 81c). For example, after the enclosed drain to the west of the building had been replaced by an open timber-lined channel, a small bath was laid in the northern room, the outlet of which fed into the drain.

The next significant development is of considerable interest since it incorporates a contraction of the property and, possibly, a decline in status in the fourth century (Fig. 81d). Post-holes were crudely dug into the once elegant mosaic floor to accommodate door-posts marking the subdivision of the southern range into separate apartments. To the south in the courtyard area, several enigmatic trenches representing robbed features or temporary drainage channels were recorded. One of them cut across one of the southern range wall lines, showing that the building had been partially demolished.

However, some time after this the area saw a significant revival (Fig. 81e). The fire-damaged northern corridor was pulled down sometime after coins, including one of Valens (AD 367–75), had been deposited there. In the east, the sub-floor of a heated room was cut through the old foundations. The main drain to the west was deliberately blocked and infilled with grey silt and rubble on both the upper and lower terraces at the same time as the southern area was levelled up. A late Roman coin (Valentinian I, AD 364–7) was found, sealed

beneath the deposits within the drain. Building 6 was rebuilt and refurbished with rooms heated by a hypocaust, of which a stoke hole and several *pilae* stacks supporting an *opus signinum* floor at $c + 4$m OD were found (Pl. 8c). At least eleven of the *pilae* tiles were stamped with a PP BR LON motif (cf Marsden 1975, 70–1), but since one of them bore traces of two distinct types of mortar, at least some of them may have been re-used. Also associated with this late Roman development was a small heated bath and an *opus signinum* lined water-tank.

The fate of this prestigious building is not known, since most of the site was horizontally truncated at this level by later activity, although one part of its *opus signinum* floor observed during the watching brief seemed to be directly overlaid by a 1m thick deposit of dark grey silts. Nevertheless, the history of this building complex has served to show that, like Building 2, most major changes were probably integral parts of a wider redevelopment; that the prosperity of the occupants is clearly reflected in the minor structural modifications; and that activity on the waterfront continued certainly until the end of the fourth century, and probably into the fifth. The latter conclusion is of considerable significance, since until recently, clear evidence of occupation in Roman London at this late date seemed to be confined to the building excavated on the old Coal Exchange site (Merrifield 1983, 255). It can now be shown that more of the harbour area was occupied in the late Roman period, and there is even evidence to suggest that the late fourth-century revival recorded on Building 6 may be paralleled on a waterfront site over 700m to the east (Butcher 1982, 101–5).

CHAPTER 12

THE HARBOUR AND THE TOWN

The previous chapters have examined the evidence to hand from the recent waterfront excavations and drawn conclusions on several distinct but related topics. In this final chapter an attempt is made to bring these separate results together, and consider some of the implications for the study of Roman London as a whole. Several books have already been written on that particular subject: Sir Mortimer Wheeler's essay was the standard work (*RCHM* 1928) until Ralph Merrifield produced his major synthesis and gazetteer (Merrifield 1965), complemented by Professor Grimes' detailed work in 1968 (Grimes 1968). The continuing archaeological work in the 1960s and 1970s generated the need for expansion and revision in the 1980s, and the books then published by Marsden and Merrifield in particular incorporated some of the new material (Marsden 1980; Merrifield 1983). However, neither of these books was able to include details of the most recent projects simply because the analysis was incomplete at the time. This unfortunate but inevitable consequence of writing major syntheses while the data gathering process is continuing (which it still is) is clearly recognised by both authors.

Nevertheless, the models they propose for the development of London support a picture which may be summarised thus: *Londinium* was founded in *c*AD 50, was devastated by the Boudican revolt in *c*AD 60 but recovered and expanded in the late first century. By *c*AD 130 a fire had destroyed much of the City but it was rebuilt, the landward defensive wall being added in *c*AD 200. However, by that date, the settlement had already begun to contract and, in spite of an early third-century revival, the fourth century saw a further decline. It is only in the interpretation of these events and in the assessment of the changing role and status of the town that the authors show differences of opinion or emphasis. The main arguments revolve around such points as whether London grew from a military or a mercantile origin; at what date was it legally recognised as a town, since the reference by

Tacitus suggests that it lacked that status in AD 60 (Merrifield 1983, 41–2), and what happened to the town in the late and sub-Roman period. Both Marsden and Merrifield agree that trade was a vital component in the life of London.

Against this broad background an interpretation of the results of recent waterfront excavations will now be presented. It is argued that the evidence considered in this book shows that the London waterfront was deliberately and vigorously expanded from *c*AD 70, rather than evolving gradually from the settlement founded in *c*AD 50. The subsequent major advances on the waterfront are also seen as the result of public, not private, initiatives. Taking this into consideration, together with an assessment of the size of London's 'commercial zone' and of its Thames valley-Watling Street hinterland, it is suggested that the town was not the most important port in the land, although it clearly played a role in the distributive network of the province.

The pattern of waterfront development

It can be shown that the first major impetus for waterfront expansion for which substantial evidence survived did not occur before *c*AD 70, demonstrably later than the Boudican revolt. However, the traces of features such as the bank and revetments on the foreshore discussed in Chapter 2 (Fig. 14a) demonstrates that the waterfront was developed in the earlier period, although subsequent disturbance makes dating and detailed interpretation difficult. The precise form the original development took was not established, but its general pattern was clearly not that of the succeeding phase, since few features can be shown to have affected the subsequent layout of the area. An implication of this could be that the earlier waterfront was a much less formal development, incorporating few masonry structures. However, arguing from such negative evidence is both difficult and dangerous. The remains of a conjectural bridge pier were discovered near Fish Street Hill but it is suggested that that structure was built in the later first century, and thus cannot represent the *first* London bridge: evidence for that may yet be found beneath Thames Street or Fish Street Hill itself.

For the crucial first period of London's history then, the evidence from the waterfront is frankly disappointing. Nevertheless, the use of the foreshore for quarrying and the relatively insubstantial non-uniform nature of the riverfront revetments stand in stark contrast to the form and scale of the subsequent pattern of activity. Whatever happened on the waterfront prior to AD 70 was quite different from that which followed.

From cAD 70–90, the timber-faced waterfront terrace, associated with an integrated system of roads, drains and buildings, was established on both sides of the bridge. It was clearly not the result of the enterprise of individual merchants but was initially part of a coordinated redevelopment of a wide area, as demonstrated in Chapter 11. The nature and scale of this project implies that it was initiated by an official body, perhaps a local town council. If so, London may have achieved *municipium* status by that stage. A date in the AD 70s for the start of this development also implies that the destruction wrought by the Boudican uprising was not made good in the waterfront area for a full decade. The broad pattern of building lines, once established by the end of the first century, seem to have been respected by much of the subsequent development. This statement would also seem to confirm the picture drawn from sites recently excavated further inland, to the west of the Walbrook stream (Perring and Roskams, forthcoming).

On the waterfront, major extensions seem to have taken place in the first century, at least twice in the second century and once in the early third but not thereafter. These developments are seen as parts of public building-works programmes, since the scale is much larger than that of the private extensions identified on the medieval waterfront (Milne and Milne 1982). Nevertheless, the Roman waterfront was not extended along its entire length at each phase: for example, there was no such development at all at the extreme western end of the frontage near Blackfriars. It was the central part of the waterfront which was extended most regularly, creating a broad, level area which contrasted with the steeply-sloping, much terraced hillside directly to the north. Urban waterfront extension is a phenomenon that has been identified in many medieval towns in Britain and on the Continent (Milne and Hobley 1981) but London is the first example of Roman date to be examined in any detail. From the first to the third century, the waterfront was advanced some 50m southwards along a considerable sector. Indeed, if the fragments of quay observed near St James Garlickhithe and south of Cannon Street Station are part of a continuous development, a maximum length of c620m for the first-century quay could be suggested.

Possible reasons suggested for such extensions are: to provide a deep water berth; to overcome the problem of silting; to maintain a sound frontage by building a new revetment on the riverwards side of a decaying face; to win land.

All of the first-century installations considered in Chapter 5, and also the third-century quay found on the St Magnus House site, were built on the inter-tidal foreshore and did not extend out as far as the deep water channel, suggesting that the establishment of a deep water berth was not the intention. It is argued in Chapter 9 that the vessels which were most suitable for work on the Roman River Thames were ones similar to the Blackfriars I ship, capable of being beached at low tide and then floated off at high tide. The accumulation of silt in the harbour on the foreshore may not have been a major problem for such versatile craft.

The first-century quays were in excellent condition when excavated, and must have been considered sound in the second century when superseded, since the line of the front wall was reused as a building foundation. The quays examined on the Pudding Lane sites did not therefore need to be replaced on structural grounds.

The fourth suggestion, to win land, seems the most consistent with the evidence to hand. To the north of the natural river bank, a steeply sloping hillside restricted development. By contrast, the waterfront extension provided a wide, level terrace which, significantly, was rapidly occupied by new buildings, particularly in the first and second centuries. That the waterfront terrace was developed as extensively as it was could imply that there was insufficient land which could be made available for such building programmes elsewhere in the town. The third-century extension is of especial interest in this regard, since it is known that a significant proportion of the urban area which was built over in the second century had been cleared by AD 200. It therefore follows that the land so cleared was not lying waste, but was being left open quite deliberately in the third century.

The decrease in the density of settlement in London in the late second century should not therefore be seen as evidence of decline, but of dramatic change (Perring, forthcoming). By the early to mid-third century, many of the timber and clay buildings in the city had been systematically removed and some were replaced by masonry structures of complex plan. Temples were restored, and much of the town was enclosed by an imposing wall. Changes were also recorded on the waterfront at this date, where the former horrea or shops and an inn (Buildings 1, 2 and 6) were transformed, presumably into domestic apartments. However, these dramatic changes and the subsequent developments give little indication of the function of the harbour in this period. The contemporary quay now lay some 35m to the south, and whatever buildings were directly connected with it lay beyond the limits of controlled excavation. Nevertheless, it is significant that no further attempt seems to have been made to advance the waterfront in the remaining c170 years of Roman rule, which contrasts noticeably with the previous pace of extension. A decrease in activity in the harbour area is implied, but the reasons for this are less certain. The changing role and smaller population of the city must obviously have had an effect. However, the construction of part of the riverside wall in the late third century provided a major physical impediment to traffic on the waterfront and must have transformed all commercial activity in the immediate area, perhaps displacing it completely. Another suggestion is that a fall in the river level in the late Roman period could have caused the tidal head to move downstream away from the city (Chapter 7), effectively removing one of the natural advantages enjoyed by the town in the first century.

The persistence of life on the waterfront has been discussed in detail in Chapter 11 and the significance of the late fourth-century revival stressed. This contributes positively to the pattern of occupation in Roman London in general, for the area of settlement in much of the rest of the city had contracted by that date. It is now possible to show that occupation continued in at least part of the town into the fifth century, but that the sixth-century activity, represented only by deposits of dark grey silt, could not be described as urban in character. Not even a prime waterfront location close to the bridge can be shown to have been continually occupied from the first century to the medieval period. This strongly suggests that the late Saxon city was a reoccupation of the site and not the direct development of a sub-Roman settlement.

The port of Roman London

The recent work on the harbour sites has also thrown new light on the role and status of London as a port in its first four centuries of life. It is argued that the Roman River Thames was tidal and that in consequence the city was not a deep-water port capable of directly accommodating vessels of the size found in the contemporary harbours outside Ostia (Chapter 9). The majority of the ships which did serve London may therefore have been vessels capable of coastal and inland waterway work, operating between the City and the major transhipment ports on the east or south-east coast. The principal ports of the province, where the largest cross-channel and seagoing ships discharged their cargoes, may well have changed during the period in question to meet specific military or economic needs, or to overcome the problems of silting and erosion. In the first and second centuries, the principal harbours may have included those big enough to have been used by the *Classis Britannica*, the Roman fleet formed specifically for coastal and cross-channel work, such as Dover, Lympne and Richborough (Philp 1980; Cleere 1977). There is little evidence to suggest that London was ever a base for this fleet. It is suggested that the principal ports of the third and fourth centuries would have been defended by some or all of the so-called Saxon Shore forts (Johnston 1977). Indeed, as Professor Cunliffe has shown, fourth-century Porchester had characteristics which were 'little different from those of a

83 *Evidence for a merchant's shrine in London? Statuette found in London in 1889. The white Carrara marble figure is a* **genius**: *around his neck are two garlands, his left hand holds a cornucopia and behind him is a ship's prow, attributes which collectively symbolise wealth gained from waterborne trade. He pours a libation from a patera onto a flaming altar while a snake, symbol of prosperity and happiness in the afterlife, grasps his wrist.*

civilian settlement' (Cunliffe 1977, 5). It could perhaps be argued that London itself should be included amongst these ports, since it too seems to have been partially refortified in the late third century (Sheldon and Tyers 1983), but there is clear evidence that the harbour installations were not renewed after that date and seem to have been allowed to decay thereafter.

To say that Roman London was a port simply implies that the town had a harbour, an area where men and merchandise were regularly transferred from ship to shore. This much has been established by the recent excavations. More penetrating questions which could be asked are how important the harbour was in the economic life of the town, how many of London's citizens made their living from harbour-related activity, and whether the Roman city was built primarily on the profits made by merchants. Any analysis of commercial activity in this period must discount modern economic concepts such as 'free trade' or 'balance of payments', which had little meaning in an ancient slave-owning economy where land was always the safest and most sought-after investment. In the classical world, 'merchants were a despised category' (Anderson 1974, 81), and much of the wealth of Roman London would have been drawn from the countryside, as was the case with most Roman towns (Anderson 1974, 19). Significantly, not one of the c70 names known from London's Roman inscriptions refers to a merchant or trader (Chapter 10). Certainly merchants and middlemen could make a living sustaining the large population of the provincial capital. Indeed, Francis Grew argues that the statue of a river god (Fig. 47) and the figure (Fig. 83) found near the Walbrook valley in c1889 (Haverfield 1906) may have been dedicated by merchants or a guild of shipowners in a shrine in London. However, the lucrative military supply contracts may not have been handled in the town, since for most of the duration of the Roman occupation the legions were based at a considerable distance from London in the north and west of the province.

On the waterfront, clear evidence of commercial buildings was only found in the areas immediately adjacent to the bridge. To the east were Buildings 1 and 2 identified as horrea (Chapters 6 and 11) and a possible pottery warehouse whose cleared contents were perhaps represented by the large third-century pottery group recovered from the St Magnus House site. To the west the position of another such store is indicated by the assemblage of burnt samian ware from the Regis House site (Chapter 2, Fig. 14d). It has also been suggested that part of Building A may have been used for storage or other waterfront-related activity for at least some of its life. However, immediately to the north and west lay Building 6 and Buildings B–F (Figs. 12, 13) which have few characteristics to suggest that they had a commercial function, with the notable exception of the fish-processing building described in Chapter 8. Excavations in 1974 showed that the area some 100m east of the Roman bridge was not extended out over the foreshore and consolidated until the mid-second century (Jones and Rhodes 1980), while the largest building known in the vicinity was a third-century town house and bath block (Marsden 1980). It therefore seems that, although the waterfront terrace was extensive, the area occupied by buildings directly related to commercial activity in the harbour may have been confined to the zone close to the bridge.

In Chapter 6, the form of the waterfront buildings is assessed, from which it is argued that a market developed on the quayside dealing in goods brought to the town by river. Such markets were also found in Rome, for example. The principal food markets in London would have been closer to the Forum on the crest of the hill to the north. The relatively modest extent of the commercial zone on the waterfront and the size of the quayside warehouses themselves combined with the evidence that the town was not a major manufacturing centre processing imported raw materials (Chapter 10) could suggest that 'trade' was not as important a component in the Roman city's life as it was in the nineteenth-century town with its sprawling docklands and industrial suburbs. The harbours and warehouses in Ostia, Portus and the Aventine were designed to meet the needs of one town, Rome (Fig. 4), with a population less than that of Britannia. If Roman London was the principal redistribution port for the whole province, then it would require facilities commensurate with that role, perhaps as large as Ostia's. The size and nature of London's harbour and warehousing as revealed so far do not support that suggestion.

Imports, exports and the hinterland of London

It is not possible to calculate the tonnage which had to be brought into Roman London to supply its daily needs or to meet the demand for luxury products not available locally, or even what proportion of the total those exotic items might have comprised. What does seem clear is that the first and second centuries in particular saw a considerable *range* of imported items coming into the town (Chapter 10). Since much of this material was of a luxury character, it is suggested that it may have been brought in primarily to satisfy the needs of the richer strata of Romano-British citizens, many of whom lived in London. The expanding town itself may therefore have been the main magnet, attracting quantities of exotic material for sale and consumption within its boundaries. Nevertheless, a proportion of the imported material would have percolated into the hinterland. An idea of the extent of the area serviced by London in this way can be gained from the study of the distribution of other major Roman towns and ports in the province. For example, the location of 43 harbours related to the road system have been identified on the English and Welsh coasts (Cleere 1978, 36), all of which could have been used to import material into the province. The distinction Dr Cleere draws between purely military and purely civilian harbours is probably academic, since a well-situated harbour could have been used for both purposes. London's hinterland would not have extended as far east as Colchester or as far south as Chichester or Canterbury, since all were served by more local ports. The hinterlands of Gloucester, Chester and Lincoln, major towns on navigable rivers, would mark the western and northern limits for the redistribution of material brought into London.

The examination of the artefacts discussed in Chapter 10 shows that there was a fundamental change in the range as well as the volume of products brought in from overseas after the mid-third century. The fate of the contemporary quay structures, which do not seem to have been replaced after that date, supports the suggestion of a marked decline in the amount of imported material coming into the town when its population was contracting. Significantly, the population of the province as a whole does not seem to have declined in the late Roman period: indeed, rural settlement seems to have expanded at this time (Taylor 1983). A major redistribution centre should presumably have prospered, but there is little evidence of expansion in London's late Roman harbour.

In Chapter 11 it was demonstrated that the major developments on the waterfront were not initiated by individual merchants but, from the late

first century, were part of a corporate plan. This suggests that the town developed the harbour, rather than developing directly from it. It therefore seems that, arguing from the archaeological evidence, the Roman harbour of London was developed to serve the considerable needs of an expanding town, but was not itself the primary cause of the town's expansion. Although some of the goods brought into London by river were redistributed in its hinterland, a major proportion was destined for the town itself. Thus, as the population declined from the late second century onwards, so did the flow of imports, although other factors may also have played a part. Roman London was never a major manufacturing centre, and thus the range of exports it would have handled was limited. There seems no cogent geographical reason why items known to have been exported from the province, such as iron from the Weald or oysters from the Thames estuary, should be transported all the way to London unless they were to be sold there. Indeed, there is ample evidence that oysters, for example, were consumed in considerable quantities in the town (Chapter 8). However, when such products were destined for export to northern Europe or the Mediterranean, they would have been handled by the coastal ports which were more conveniently situated for this traffic.

Roman London should not therefore be seen as a port developed primarily by merchants (cf Marsden 1980) and there is no evidence at all to substantiate Dr Morris' claim that '*Londinium* was a large and busy port, probably handling more tonnage than any other port in Roman Europe' (Morris 1982, 162). Its harbour contributed to the life of the city, enabling the provincial settlement to maintain the appearance and lifestyle of a substantial Roman town. However, the nature and development of the installations themselves show that the harbour was not the *raison d'être* of the town, particularly in the third and fourth centuries. Certainly London played an important role in the distributive network of the province, acting as a market centre for its hinterland, as did the other major towns: London was *a*, not *the*, Romano–British port. This suggestion may seem to be at variance with the oft-quoted (and misquoted) statement by Tacitus, referred to in the Preface. However, rather than appraising the archaeological evidence in the light of such documentary references as there are for Roman London (*RCHM*

1928, 1–7), it is suggested that those references should be reconsidered in the light of the material evidence.

Roman London was, however, ideally situated as an administrative centre, lying at the junction of several tribal boundaries on a major navigable waterway crossed by a bridge from which roads radiated out to the capitals of the Cantiaci and the Regnenses to the south, the Atrebates to the west and the Catuvellauni and Trinovantes to the north and east (Fig. 84). The importance of the bridge to this network cannot be stressed too highly (Chap-

ter 4). Certainly the town would have needed its quays, its waterfront market, its warehouses to help meet its daily needs, but the ultimate fate of the settlement would be more directly linked with the organisation and reorganisation of the province, rather than with economic or mercantile issues.

Roman London: a tale of three cities

Combining the evidence from the waterfront excavations with that from the recent inland sites (eg Roskams 1978, 1980; Perring 1981), it can be

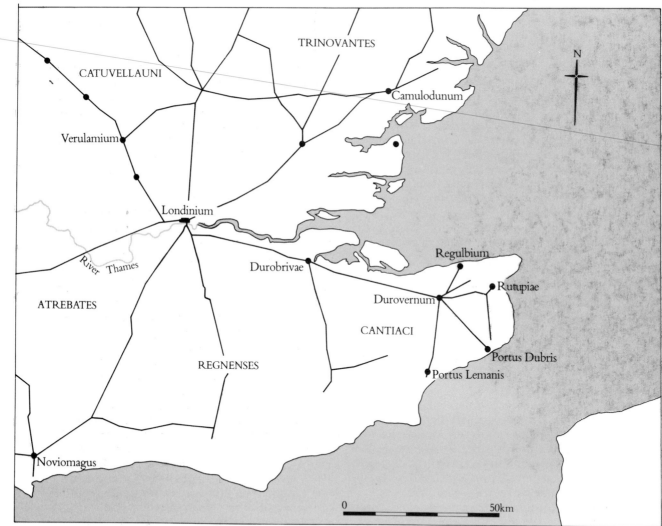

84 *Roman London as a communications centre, sitting on the lowest bridging point of a major navigable river, with roads radiating from it to the tribal capitals.*

argued that there are at least three distinct phases in the town's development. The earliest phase, cAD 50–70, was least well-preserved on the waterfront, but it seems that the settlement grew somewhat haphazardly at the junction of the road network and the navigable Thames, rather than as a carefully-planned new town. However, Marsden suggests that this early town was planned (Marsden 1980, 17–26), although Merrifield argues that 'no proper judgement can be made on the nature of the first occupation of London from this scanty evidence' (Merrifield 1983, 43).

The second phase, from the late first to the late second centuries, saw the imposition of a far more integrated formal layout, both in the harbour area and elsewhere in the town, which was developed through a series of public building programmes. This second London expanded briskly as a major administrative centre. Although imports certainly poured into the town and some were redistributed into its hinterland, most were destined for its large population: in this period, London was a Westminster, not a Tilbury.

The major transformation in the third century was also reflected on the waterfront. Although the population of London was clearly smaller, it was still wealthy, as the substantial nature of the rebuilding shows. In spite of several reversals, it continued to flourish into the fifth century.

London and the study of provincial Roman harbours

In 1978, the report on the third-century quay at Caerleon stated that 'little is known of Roman ports in this country: fortunately that little has been admirably summarised by J. Fryer (1973) who thus relieves us of the need to do likewise' (Boon 1978, 2). The summaries published subsequently (Cleere 1978; Milne and Hobley 1981) show that little progress has been made since then. This emphasises the importance of the recent waterfront work in London, where the sequence, date, extent and nature of the harbour installations has been examined more closely than has been possible elsewhere. It is surprising that more effort has not been expended on this topic nationally, since the sites are clearly very rewarding, providing evidence of civil engineering, boat building,

river and sea-level change and settlement history, quite apart from harbour installations and trade patterns. It is argued that the Roman harbour in London was not necessarily the largest in the province, and may therefore be typical of waterfront development in many coastal or riparian towns. It follows that many of the more general statements made in this report could be applicable to other Romano–British towns, as work in Caerleon and Dover (Rigold 1969) confirms. Indeed, the discoveries at Xanten in Germany (Petrikovitz 1952) and Pommeroeul in Belgium (de Boe 1978) for example show that similar developments can be expected elsewhere in northern Europe. London may only be exceptional in that the relevant sites became available for study, ie were about to be destroyed, at the same time as generous financial assistance could be negotiated to facilitate their recording. The implications are obvious for archaeologists in other towns where waterfront development is threatened.

This report on a neglected area of study, the development of London's Roman harbour, has attempted to show how rich the waterfront deposits are and how important their analysis is to an understanding of the City's history in particular and Roman harbours in general. Clearly much more excavation and research is required before definitive statements on either topic can be made, but it is hoped that the evidence considered in this book has made a positive contribution to that end.

The late twentieth century saw the City develop as a banking and financial centre as it swept away the fish market, the docks and the riverside warehouses of the nineteenth-century port. It is now known that this major transformation of London is just one of the many it has undergone since its initial foundation in cAD 50. For pedestrians in Lower Thames Street today there is nothing to remind them of the harbour that once served the provincial capital of Britannia, save for a decayed baulk of wood imprisoned in the forecourt of the church of St Magnus the Martyr, and the name of the new building opposite. This is called Centurion House, an acknowledgement of the discoveries made just before its construction during the latest redevelopment of the London waterfront.

BIBLIOGRAPHY

INDEX

BIBLIOGRAPHY

AKEROYD, A., 1972, 'Archaeological and Historical Evidence for Subsidence in Southern Britain', *Phil. Trans. Royal. Soc. Lond.*, *272*, 151–69

ALZON, C., 1965, *Problèmes relatifs à la location des entrepôts en droit romain*

ANDERSON, P., 1974, *Passages from antiquity to feudalism*

ARMITAGE, P., WEST, B. and STEEDMAN, K., 1984, 'New evidence of Black Rat in Roman London', *Lond. Arch.*, *4*, No 14, 375–82

ARTHUR, P., forthcoming, 'Roman amphorae and the Ager Falernus under the Empire', *Pap. British School Rome*

ASTOLFI, F., GUIDOBALDI, F. and PRONTI, A., 1978, 'Horrea Agrippiana', *Archeologia Classica*, *30*, 31–107

AUDIN, A., 1972, 'Un quartier commercial' *Archeologia*, *50*

BAILLE, M., 1982, *Tree-ring dating and archaeology*

BARKER, P., 1977, *Techniques of archaeological excavation*

BATEMAN, N., and LOCKER, A., 1982 'The Sauce of the Thames' *Lond. Arch.*, *4*, No 8, 204–7

BATEMAN, N. and MILNE, G., 1983, 'A Roman harbour in London', *Britannia*, *14*, 207–26

BATTARBEE, R., 1979, 'Diatoms in lake sediments', in Berglund, B. (ed), 1979, *Palaeo-hydrological change in the temperate zone in the last 15,000 years: lake and mire environments*, 177–226

BATTARBEE, R., 1983, *Diatom analysis of River Thames foreshore deposits . . . at Pudding Lane, London*, Working Papers in Palaeoecology, *2*

BAUER, H., 1978, 'Un tentativo di riconstruzione degli Horrea Agrippiana', *Archeologia Classica* *30*, 132–46

BEAVIS, J., 1970, 'Some aspects of the use of Purbeck marble in Roman Britain', *Proc. Dorset Nat. Hist. and Arch. Soc.*, *92*, 181–204

BECKER, B., 1981, 'Fällungsdaten Römischer Bauhölzer', *Fundberichte aus Baden-Wurttemburg*, *6*, 369–86

BENOIT, F., 1957, 'Observations sur les cryptoportiques d'Arles' *Rivista di Studi Liguri*, *23*, 107

BENTLEY, D. and PRITCHARD, F., 1982, 'The Roman Cemetery at St Bartholomew's Hospital', *Trans. L.A.M.A.S.*, *33*, 134–72

BIDDLE, M., HUDSON, D.M. and HEIGHWAY, C.M., 1973, *The Future of London's Past*

BIRD, J., CHAPMAN, H. and CLARK, J. (eds), 1978, *Collectanea Londoniensia, Studies in London archaeology and history presented to Ralph Merrifield*, L.A.M.A.S. Special Paper No 2

BIRLEY, A.R., 1979, *The People of Roman Britain*

BLACKMAN, D., 1973, 'Evidence of Sea-level Change in Ancient Harbours and Coastal Installations', in Blackman (ed), *Marine Archaeology*, 115–39

BLACKMAN, D., (ed) 1973, *Marine Archaeology*, Colston Papers, *23*

BOON, G., 1978, 'Excavations on the site of a Roman quay at Caerleon', in Boon, G. (ed), 1978, *Monographs and Collections, 1, Roman Sites*, Cambrian Arch. Assoc., 1–24

BOSTOCK, J. and RILEY, H.T. (eds), 1855, *Natural History by Pliny the Elder*

BOYD, P., 1981, 'The micropalaeontology and palaeoecology of medieval estuarine sediments from the Fleet and Thames', in Neale and Brazier (eds), 1981, *Microfossils from recent and fossil shelf seas*, 274–292

BROTHWELL, D., and BROTHWELL, P., 1969, *Food in Antiquity. A Survey of the Diet of Early Peoples*

BRUNT, P., 1980, 'Free Labour and Public Works at Rome', *J.R.S.*, *70*, 81–100

BURNHAM, B.C., and JOHNSON, H.B., 1979, *Invasion and Response. The case of Roman Britain*, B.A.R. *73*

BUTCHER, S., 1982, 'The Excavation of a Roman Building on the east side of the White Tower 1956–7', in Parnell, 1982, 101–4

CAFARELLI, E. and CAPUTO, G., 1966, *The Buried City: excavations at Leptis Magna*

CALLENDER, M., 1965, *Roman Amphorae*

CARY, M. and SCULLARD, H.H., 1975, *A History of Rome*

CASSON, L., 1965, 'Harbour and River Boats of Ancient Rome', *J.R.S.*, *55*, 31–9

CHARLESWORTH, D., 1966, 'Roman Square Bottles', *Journ. Glass Stud.*, 8, 26–40

CLARKE, J.G.D., 1954, *Excavations at Starr Carr*

CLEERE, H., 1977, 'The Classis Britannica' in Johnston (ed), 1977, 16–19

CLEERE, H., 1978, 'Roman harbours in Britain south of Hadrian's Wall', in du Plat Taylor and Cleere (eds), 1978, 36–40

COLE, H., 1956, *Oyster Cultivation in Britain. A manual of current practice*

COLES, J. (ed), 1975–83, *Somerset Levels Papers*, 1–9

CONSTANS, L.A., 1921, *Arles Antique*

COSTE, M., 1861, *Voyage d'Exploration sur le Littoral de la France et de l'Italie*

CROAD, S., 1983, *London's bridges*, R.C.H.M.

CUNLIFFE, B., 1968, *Fifth report on the excavation of the Roman fort at Richborough, Kent*, Soc. Antiq. Res. Rep., 23

CUNLIFFE, B., 1971, *Excavations at Fishbourne 1961–1969 – Vol 1: The Site.*, Soc. Antiq. Res. Rep., 26

CUPPERS, H., 1969, *Die Trier Römerbrücken*

D'ARMS, J.H., 1981, *Commerce and Social Standing in Ancient Rome*

DE BOE, G., 1978, 'Roman boats from a small river harbour at Pommeroeul, Belgium', in du Plat Taylor and Cleere (eds), 1978, 22–30

DE RUYT, C., 1983, *Macellum. Marche Alimentaire des Romains*

DE WEERD, M., 1978, 'Ships of the Roman period at Zwammerdam/Nigrum Pullum, Germania Inferior', in du Plat Taylor and Cleere (eds), 1978, 15–21

DEPARTMENT OF TRANSPORT, 1982, *Port Statistics*

DETSICAS, A.P., 1967, 'Excavations at Eccles, 1966', *Arch. Cant.*, 82, 162–78

DEVOY, R., 1979, 'Flandrian sea-level changes and vegetational history of the Lower Thames Estuary', *Phil. Trans. R. Soc. Lond. B*, 285, 355–407

DEVOY, R., 1980, 'Post glacial environmental change and man in the Thames estuary: a synopsis', in Thompson (ed), 1980, 134–48

DOHERGUE, C., 1966, 'Un envoi de lampes du potier *Caius Clodius*', *Melanges Casa Velasquez*, 2, 5–40

D'OLIER, B., 1972, 'Subsidence and sea-level rise in the Thames estuary', *Phil. Trans. R. Soc. London. A*, 272, 121–30

DOWKER, G., 1882, 'A Roman Villa at Wingham', *Arch. Cant.*, 14, 134–9

DRURY, P. (ed), 1982, *Structural Reconstruction: approaches to the interpretation of the excavated remains of buildings*, B.A.R. 110

DU PLAT TAYLOR, J. and CLEERE, H. (eds), 1978, *Roman shipping and trade: Britain and the Rhine provinces*, C.B.A. Res. Rep., 24

DUNHAM, K., 1972, 'The evidence for subsidence', *Phil. Trans. R. Soc. Lond. A*, 272, 81–6

DYSON, T. and SCHOFIELD, J., 1981, 'Excavations in the City of London: Second Interim Report, 1974–8.' *Trans. L.A.M.A.S.*, 32, 24–81

ELLMERS, D., 1978, 'Shipping on the Rhine during the Roman period: the pictorial evidence' in du Plat Taylor and Cleere (eds), 1978, 1–14

EUZENNAT, M. and SALVIAT, F., 1968, *Les découverts archaeologiques de la Bourse a Marseille*

EVANS, J., forthcoming, in Limbrey and Greig, *Excavations at New Palace Yard, Westminster*

EVERARD, C., 1980, 'On sea-level changes', in Thompson (ed), 1980, 1–23

FEDER, T, 1978, *Great treasures of Pompeii and Herculaneum*

FEHR, H., 1981, 'Eine Rheinbrücke zwischen Koblenz und Ehrenbreitstein aus der Regierungszeit des Claudius', *Bonner Jahrbuch.*, 181, 287–300

FLETCHER, J., 1982, 'The waterfront of *Londinium*: The date of the Quays at the Custom House Site Reassessed', *Trans. L.A.M.A.S.*, 33, 79–84

FLOWER, B. and ROSENBAUM, E., 1958, *Apicius: the Roman cookery book*

FLOWER, B. and ROSENBAUM, E., 1980, *The Roman Cookery Book*

FRERE, S., 1967, *Britannia*

FRYER, J., 1973, 'The harbour installations of Roman Britain', in Blackman, D. (ed), 1973, 261–73

FULFORD, M., 1978, 'The interpretation of Britain's late Roman trade: the scope of medieval historical and archaeological analogy' in du Plat Taylor and Cleere (eds), 1978, 59–69

GAYRAUD, M., 1981, 'Narbonne antique des origines a la fin du IIIe siecle', *Revue Archeologique de Narbonnaise*, 8

GENTLEMAN'S MAGAZINE, 1834, I (Jan), 'Roman Bath Discovered near the Monument, London', 95–6

GENTRY, A., 1976, *Roman military stone built granaries in Britain*, B.A.R., 32

GRAHAM, A., 1978, 'The geology of north Southwark and its topographical development in the post-Pleistocene period', in Bird, Chapman and Clark (eds), 1978, 501–17

GRANGER-TAYLOR, H., 1982, 'Weaving clothes to shape in the ancient world: the tunic and toga of the Arringatore', *Textile History*, 13.1, 3–25

GRANT, M., (ed), 1956, *Tacitus: the annals of Imperial Rome*

GREEN, C.M., 1980, 'The Roman Pottery' in Jones and Rhodes, 1980, 39–79

GREENSMITH, J., and TOOLEY, M., (eds), 1982, 'Report on IGCP Project 61, sealevel movements during the last deglacial hemicycle', *Proc. Geol. Ass*, *93*, 1–125

GREENSMITH, J., and TUCKER, E., 1973, 'Holocene transgressions and regressions on the Essex coast outer Thames estuary' *Geol. en Mijnb.*, *52*, (4), 193–202

GRIMES, W.F., 1968, *The Excavation of Roman and Mediaeval London*

GROSE, D.F., 1977, 'Early Blown Glass: the western evidence', *Journ. Glass Stud.*, *19*, 9–29

GUNTHER, R., 1897, *The Oyster Culture of the Ancient Romans*

HANSON, W., 1978, 'The Organisation of Roman Military Timber-Supply', *Britannia*, *9*, 293–305

HARDEN, D.B., 1947, 'The Glass' in Hawkes, C.F.C. and Hull, M.R., 1947, *Camulodunum*, Rep. Res. Comm. Soc. Antiq. Lond., *14*, 287–307

HASSALL, M., 1978, 'Britain and the Rhine Provinces: epigraphic evidence for Roman trade' in du Plat Taylor and Cleere (eds), 1978, 41–8

HENIG, M., forthcoming, 'A cache of Roman intaglios from Eastcheap, City of London', *Trans. L.A.M.A.S.*, *35*

HIGGINS, R.A., 1967, *Greek Terracottas*

HILL, C., MILLET, M. and BLAGG, T., 1980, *The Roman Riverside Wall and Monumental Arch in London, Excavations at Baynard's Castle, Upper Thames Street, London, 1974–76*, L.A.M.A.S. Special Paper No 3

HILLAM, J., 1980, 'A Mediaeval oak tree-ring Chronology for South-east England', *Tree Ring Bulletin*, *40*, 13–22

HILLAM, J., 1981, 'An English Tree-ring Chronology AD 404–1216', *Med. Arch.*, *25*, 31–44

HILLAM, J., and MORGAN, R., 1981, 'What value is dendrochronology to waterfront archaeology?', in Milne and Hobley (eds), 1981, 39–46

HOBLEY, B. and SCHOFIELD, J., 1977, 'Excavations in the City of London, First Interim Report, 1974–5.' *Ant. Journ.*, *57*, 31–66

HOLLSTEIN, E., 1980, *Mitteleuropaische Eichenchronologie*

HOPKINS, K., 1980, 'Taxes and Trade in the Roman Empire (200 BC–AD 400)', *J.R.S.*, *70*, 101–25

HOUSTON, G.W., 1980, 'The administration of Italian seaports during the three centuries of the Roman Empire' in d'Arms, J.H. and Kopf, E.C.

(eds), 1980, *The seaborne commerce of Ancient Rome*, M.A.A.R., *36*, 157–72

HULL, M., 1958, *Roman Colchester*

HUSTEDT, F., 1957, 'Die Diatomeenflora des Fluss-systems der Weser im Gebiet der Hansestadt Bremen', *Abh. Naturw. Von Bremen*, *34*, 181–440

JACKSON, D. and AMBROSE, T., 1976, 'A Roman timber Bridge at Aldwincle, Northants', *Britannia*, *7*, 39–52

JACKSON, G., 1983, *The History and Archaeology of Ports*

JENKINS, F., 1958, 'The Cult of the "Pseudo-Venus" in Kent', *Arch. Cant.*, *72*, 60–76

JENKINS, F., 1978, 'Some interesting types of clay statuettes of the Roman period found in London', in Bird, Chapman and Clark (eds), 1978

JOHNSTON, D. (ed), 1977, *The Saxon Shore*, C.B.A. Res. Rep., *18*

JONES, A.H.M., 1973, *The Later Roman Empire*

JONES, D.M. and RHODES, M., 1980, *Excavations on the site of Billingsgate Buildings, Lower Thames Street*, L.A.M.A.S. Special Paper No 4

KENWARD, H.K. and WILLIAMS, D., 1979, 'Biological evidence for the Roman warehouse in Coney St', *Y.A.T.*, *14*, No 2

LAING, D., 1818, *The New Custom House, London*

LAMBERT, F., 1921, 'Some Recent Excavations in London', *Arch.*, *71*, 55–112

LIVERSIDGE, J., 1976, 'Woodwork' in Brown, D. (ed), 1976, *Roman Crafts*, 154–65

LOCKER, A., 1983, *The fish bones from Area A, PEN 79 (Peninsula House)*. Unpublished archive report, HBMC

MALONEY, C., 1982, 'Copthall Avenue', *Pop. Arch.*, *3*, No 12, 32–5

MALONEY, J., 1983, 'Recent work on London's defences', in Maloney, J., and Hobley, B. (eds), *Roman Urban Defences in the West*, C.B.A. Res. Rep., *51*, 96–117

MANNING, W.H., 1975a, 'Economic influences on land use in the military areas of the Highland Zone during the Roman period', in Evans, J.G., Limbrey, S. and Cleere, H. (eds.), 1975, *The effect of man on the landscape: the Highland Zone*, C.B.A. Res. Rep., *11*, 112–16

MANNING, W.H., 1975b, 'Roman military timber granaries', *Saalburg Jahrbuch*, *32*, 105–29

MARSDEN, P., 1965a, 'The County Hall Ship', *Trans. L.A.M.A.S.*, *21*, 109–17

MARSDEN, P., 1965b, 'A Boat of the Roman Period Discovered on the Site of New Guy's House, Bermondsey, 1958', *Trans. L.A.M.A.S.*, *21*, 118–31

MARSDEN, P., 1967, *A Ship of the Roman Period from Blackfriars, in the City of London*

MARSDEN, P., 1975, 'The Excavation of a Roman Palace Site in London, 1961–1972', *Trans. L.A.M.A.S.*, *26*, 1–102

MARSDEN, P., 1976, 'Two Roman Public Baths in London', *Trans. L.A.M.A.S.*, *27*, 2–70

MARSDEN, P., 1977, 'Celtic ships of Europe', in McGrail (ed), 1977, 281–288

MARSDEN, P., 1978, 'The Discovery of the Civic Centre of Roman London', in Bird, Chapman and Clark (eds), 1978, 89–103

MARSDEN, P., 1980, *Roman London*

MARSDEN, P., 1981, 'Shipping and the waterfronts of London', in Milne and Hobley (eds), 1981, 10–16

MARSH, G., 1981, 'London's samian supply and its relationship to the development of the Gallic samian industry: Appendix 1', in Anderson, A.C. and Anderson, A.S. (eds), *Roman pottery research in Britain and North West Europe*, B.A.R. Int. Ser., *123(i)*, 221–4

MATTHEWS, J.F., 1975, *Western Aristocracies and Imperial Court*

MCGRAIL, S. (ed), 1977, *Sources and Techniques in Boat Archaeology*, B.A.R., *29*

MCGRAIL, S., 1978, *Logboats of England and Wales*, B.A.R., *51*

MCGRAIL, S. (ed), 1982, *Woodworking Techniques before AD 1500*, B.A.R., *129*

MCGRAIL, S., and SWITSUR, R., 1979, 'Mediaeval log boats', *Med. Arch.*, *23*, 229–31

MEIGGS, R., 1973, *Roman Ostia*

MEIGGS, R., 1982, *Trees and Timber in the Ancient Mediterranean World*

MENSCHING, E., 1981, 'Die Koblenzer Rheinbrücker, P. Pomponius Secundus und der Brückenbau an Rhein und Mosel', *Bonner Jahrbuch*, *188*, 325–54

MERRIFIELD, R., 1965, *The Roman City of London*

MERRIFIELD, R., 1983, *London: City of the Romans*

MERRIFIELD, R. and SHELDON, H., 1974, 'Roman London Bridge: a view from both banks', *Lond. Arch.*, *2*, No 8, 183–91

MILLER, L., 1982, 'Miles Lane: the early Roman Waterfront', *Lond. Arch.*, *4*, No 6, 143–7

MILLER, L., SCHOFIELD, J., and RHODES, M., forthcoming, *The Roman Quay at St Magnus House*, L.A.M.A.S. Special Paper

MILLS, P., 1980, 'Excavations at Cromwell Green in the Palace of Westminster', *Trans. L.A.M.A.S.*, *31*, 18–28

MILNE, G., 1982, 'Further Evidence for Roman London Bridge?', *Britannia*, *13*, 271–6

MILNE, G., forthcoming, 'The development of London's Roman harbour' in A.E. Herteig (ed), proceedings of the Second International Conference on Waterfront Archaeology

MILNE, G., BATTARBEE, R., STRAKER, V., and YULE, B., 1983, 'The London Thames in the mid-first century', *Trans. L.A.M.A.S.* *34*, 19–30

MILNE, G. and HOBLEY, B. (eds), 1981, *Waterfront Archaeology in Britain and Northern Europe*

MILNE, G. and MILNE, C., 1979, 'The making of the London waterfront', *Current Arch.*, *66*, 198–204

MILNE, G. and MILNE, C., 1982, *Medieval waterfront development at Trig Lane, London*, L.A.M.A.S. Special Paper No 5

MORRIS, J., 1982, *Londinium: London in the Roman Empire*

MORRIS, P., 1979, *Agricultural buildings in Roman Britain*, B.A.R., *70*

MUCKLEROY, K., 1978, *Maritime Archaeology*

MUSEE D'HISTOIRE DE MARSEILLE, 1979, *Naissance d'une ville: Marseille*

NUNN, P., 1983, 'The development of the River Thames in central London during the Flandrian', *Trans. Inst. Brit. Geographers*, *8*, 187–213

PARKER, A.J., 1973, 'Appendix A: Catalogue of shipwrecks', *Nautical and archaeological evidence for the social and economic history of Roman Spain, especially Baetica, under the early empire*, D. Phil, Oxford

PARNELL, G., 1977, 'Excavations at the Tower of London, 1976–7', *Lond. Arch.*, *3*, No 4, 97–9

PARNELL, G., 1978, 'An earlier Roman Riverside Wall at the Tower of London', *Lond. Arch.*, *3*, No 4, 171–6

PARNELL, G., 1982, 'The Excavation of the Roman City Wall at the Tower of London and Tower Hill, 1954–76', *Trans. L.A.M.A.S.*, *33*, 85–133

PEACOCK, D.P.S., 1978, 'The Rhine and the problem of Gaulish wine in Roman Britain', in du Plat Taylor and Cleere (eds), 1978, 49–57

PERRING, D., 1981, 'Excavations at Watling Court, Part 1: Roman', *Lond. Arch.*, *4*, No 4, 103–8

PERRING, D., and ROSKAMS, S., forthcoming, *Roman development in London, west of the Walbrook*, L.A.M.A.S. Special Paper

PETRIKOVITZ, H von, 1952, 'Die ausgrabungen in der Colonia Traiana bei Xanten', *Bonner Jahrb.*, *152*, 145–57

PHILP, B.J., 1977, 'The Forum of Roman London: Excavations of 1968–9', *Britannia*, *8*, 1–64

PHILP, B., 1981, *The excavation of the Roman forts of the Classis Britannica at Dover 1970–77*

PHILPOTS, J.R., 1890, *Oysters and all about them*

PILCHER, J., BAILLE, M., SCHMIDT, B., and BECKER, B., 1984, 'A 7272-year tree-ring chronology for western Europe', *Nature, 312*, 150–52

P.L.A., 1982, *Port of London Authority: handbook of tide tables*

PONSICH, M. and TARRADELL, M., 1965, *Garum et Industries Antiques de Salaisons dans la Mediteranee Occidentale*

PRICE, J.E., 1870, 'Reminiscences of the Steel-yard formerly in Upper Thames Street', *Trans. L.A.M.A.S., 3*, 67–78

PRICE, J., 1978, 'Trade in Glass' in du Plat Taylor and Cleere (eds), 1978, 70–78

PRITCHARD, F.A., forthcoming, 'Ornamental stonework from Roman London', *Britannia, 17*

PUDNEY, J., 1975, *London's Docks*

RACKHAM, D., BLAIR, W. and MUNBY, J., 1978, 'The thirteenth-century roofs and floor of the Blackfriars Priory at Gloucester', *Med. Arch., 22*, 105–22

R.C.H.M., 1928, Royal Commission on Historical Monuments (England): *An Inventory of the Historical Monuments in London, III, Roman London*

RICHARDSON, B., forthcoming, 'The Roman pottery', in Miller, *et al*, forthcoming

RICHMOND, I., 1961, 'Roman timber building' in Jope, E., 1961, *Studies in Building History*, 15–26

RICHTER, G.M.A., 1955, *Ancient Italy*

RICKMAN, G., 1971, *Roman granaries and store buildings*

RICKMAN, G., 1980, *The corn supply of ancient Rome*

RIGOLD, S., 1969, 'The Roman Haven of Dover', *Arch. Journ., 126*, 78–100

RIGOLD, S., 1975, 'Structural aspects of mediaeval timber bridges', *Med. Arch., 19*, 48–91

ROACH SMITH, C., 1859, *Illustrations of Roman London*

ROSKAMS, S., 1978, 'The Milk Street Excavation', *Lond. Arch., 3*, No 8, 199–204

ROSKAMS, S., 1980, 'G.P.O. Newgate Street, 1975–9: the Roman levels', *Lond. Arch., 3*, No 15, 403–7

ROSKAMS, S. and WATSON, L., 1981, 'The Hadrianic Fire of London – a reassessment of the evidence', *Lond. Arch., 4*, No 3, 62–5

ROUGE, J., 1966, *Réchérchés sur l'Organisation du Commerce Maritime en Mediterranée sous l'Empire Romain*

SALVIAT, F., 1972, 'Marseille', *Gallia, 30*, 520–4

SALWAY, P., 1982, *Roman Britain*

SANQUER, R. and GALLIOU, P., 1972, 'Garum, Sel, et Salaisons en Armorique Gallo-Romaine', *Gallia, 30*, 199–223.

SCHIEFERDECKER, F.D., 1981, 'Brücken-bautechnische Überlegungen zur römerzeit-lichen Rheinbrücke bei Koblenz', *Bonner Jahrbuch, 118*, 313–24

SCHOFIELD, A.F. (ed), 1959, *On the Characteristics of Animals by Aelian, 3*, Bk XII

SCHOFIELD, J. and DYSON, T. (eds), 1980, *Archaeology of the city of London*

SEALEY, P.R., and DAVIES, G.M.R., forthcoming, 'Falernian wine at Roman Colchester', *Britannia*

SHELDON, H., 1974, Excavations at Toppings and Sun Wharves, Southwark', *Trans. L.A.M.A.S., 25*, 1–116

SHELDON, H., and TYERS, I., 1983, 'Recent dendrochronological work in Southwark and its implications', *Lond. Arch., 4*, No 13, 355–61

SHIRLEY SMITH, H., 1953, *The world's great bridges*

STACCIOLI, R., 1954, 'I criptoportici forensi di Aosta e di Arles', *Rendiconti della classe di Scienza Morali, Storiche e Filologique dell' Accademie dei Lincei, 9*, 645

STOW, J., 1970, *A Survey of London*, Everyman edition

STRAKER, V., 1984, 'First and Second century carbonised grain from Roman London' in Zeist, W. van, and Casparie, W. (eds), *Plants and Ancient Man*, 323–9

STRICKLAND, T.J. and WARD, S., 1981, 'Chester', in Milne and Hobley (eds), 1981, 105–6

TATTON-BROWN, T., 1974, 'Excavations at the Custom House Site, City of London, 1973', *Trans. L.A.M.A.S., 25*, 117–219

TATTON-BROWN, T., 1975, 'Excavations at the Custom House Site, City of London, 1973; part 2', *Trans. L.A.M.A.S., 26*, 103–70

TAYLOR, C., 1983, *Village and Farmstead*

TESTAGUZZA, O., 1964, 'The Port of Rome', *Archaeology, 17*, 173–9

THOMAS, E.B., 1964, *Römische Villen in Pannonien*

THOMPSON, F. (ed), 1980, *Archaeology and coastal change*, Soc. Antiq. Occ. Pap., 1

ULBERT, G., 1959, 'Römische Holzfässer aus Regensburg', *Bayersiche Vorgeschichtsblätter, 24*, 6–29

VINCE, A., 1984, 'The Aldwych: Mid-Saxon London discovered?', *Current Arch., 93*, 310–12

VITELLI, G., 1980, 'Grain storage and urban growth in Imperial Ostia: a quantative study', *World Arch., 12*, No 1, 54–68

WACHER, J., 1975, *The Towns of Roman Britain*

WADDINGTON, W., 1931, *The story of the site of Regis House, King William Street, London, E.C.4*

WARD-PERKINS, J.B., 1980, 'Nicomedia and the marble trade', *Pap. British School Rome*, *48*, 23–69

WEEKS, J., 'Roman Carpentry Joints: Adoption and Adaption' in McGrail (ed), 1982, 157–68

WEST, R., 1972, 'Relative land-sea level changes in south-eastern England during the Pleistocene', *Phil. Trans. R. Soc. Lond. A*, *272*, 87–98

WHEELER, A., 1978, *Key to the Fishes of Northern Europe*

WHEELER, A., 1979, *The Tidal Thames*

WHITE, K.D., 1982, *Greek and Roman Technology*

WHITTAKER, C.R., 1983, 'Late Roman Trade and Traders' in Garnsey, P., Hopkins, K., and Whittaker, C.R. (eds), 1983, *Trade in the Ancient Economy*, 163–180

WILD, J.P., 1970, *Textile Manufacture in the Northern Roman Provinces*

WILD, J.P., 1975, 'Roman textiles from the Walbrook (London)', *Germania*, *53*, 138–43

WILD, J.P., 1978, 'Cross-channel trade and the textile industry' in du Plat Taylor and Cleere (eds), 1978, 79–81

WILD, J.P., 1979, 'Roman and native in textile technology' in Burnham and Johnson (eds), 1979, 123–31

WILLCOX, G., 1975, 'Problems and possible conclusions related to the history and archaeology of the Thames in the London region', *Trans. L.A.M.A.S.*, *26*, 285–92

WILLIAMS, T., 1982, 'St Peters Hill', *Pop. Arch.*, *4*, No 1, 24–30

WILMOTT, A., 1982, 'Excavations at Queen Street, City of London, 1953 and 1960, and Roman timber-lined wells in London', *Trans. L.A.M.A.S.*, *33*, 1–78

INDEX

Page numbers in italics refer to pages on which illustrations appear; those in bold refer to colour photographs